Growing Your Faith
by Giving It Away

Telling the

Gospel Story

with Grace

and Passion

R. York Moore

InterVarsity Press
Downers Grove, Illinois

InterVarsity Press
P.O. Box 1400, Downers Grove, IL 60515-1426
World Wide Web: www.ivpress.com
E-mail: mail@ivpress.com

InterVarsity Press® is the book-publishing division of InterVarsity Christian Fellowship/USA®, a student movement active on campus at hundreds of universities, colleges and schools of nursing in the United States of America, and a member movement of the International Fellowship of Evangelical Students. For information about local and regional activities, write Public Relations Dept., InterVarsity Christian Fellowship/USA, 6400 Schroeder Rd., P.O. Box 7895, Madison, WI 53707-7895, or visit the IVCF website at <www.intervarsity.org>.

All Scripture quotations, unless otherwise indicated, are taken from the New American Standard Bible®, copyright 1960, 1962, 1963, 1968, 1971, 1972, 1973, 1975, 1977, 1995 by The Lockman Foundation. Used by permission.

Design: Cindy Kiple
Images: PIER/Getty Images

ISBN 0-8308-3262-9

Printed in the United States of America ∞

Library of Congress Cataloging-in-Publication Data

Moore, R. York, 1969-
  Growing your faith by giving it away: telling the Gospel story with
grace and passion / by R. York Moore.
    p. cm.
  Includes bibliographical references.
  ISBN 0-8308-3262-9 (pbk.: alk. paper)
  1. Witness bearing (Christianity) 2. Evangelistic work. I. Title.
  BV4520.M57 2005
  248'.5—dc22

                                                                    2005004492

P 19 18 17 16 15 14 13 12 11 10 9 8 7 6 5 4 3 2 1
Y 19 18 17 16 15 14 13 12 11 10 09 08 07 06 05

To my heavenly Daddy

for taking the time to build sandcastles with me.

They may come and go, but your love lasts forever.

Thank you, Daddy.

CONTENTS

INTRODUCTION
The Lost Adventure

Do not leave your bags unattended or receive packages from strangers." The voice over the loudspeaker boomed through the terminal as I sank into the soft leather-upholstered chair. I was on my way home to Detroit after a trip to Jamaica and had a layover in Miami, so I decided to do some work on my laptop. The clickity-clack of the keys didn't seem right without a cup of coffee by my side, so I ventured over to the Starbucks vendor. I had lost nearly fifty pounds on the Atkins diet, but this was before the low-carb craze had swept the nation, so few pre-made alternatives were available on restaurant and coffee shop menus. I asked the woman behind the counter, "What do you have that's low in carbohydrates?"

"You're on that Atkins diet, aren't you?" she demanded.

I sheepishly answered that I was, and she began to rattle off my low-carb options. I immediately felt the need, as I often had before, for one of those Star Trek universal translators to help me decipher the Starbuckian language. The conversation went something like this:

Starbuckian Jedi Master: "You would love a breve latte."

Me: "A brevy what?"

Starbuckian Jedi Master: "It's a latte—espresso with steamed milk—made with half-and-half. Very low in carbs!"

Me: "Can I get that in a decaf?"

Starbuckian Jedi Master: "Sure, what size?"

Me: "Large."

Starbuckian Jedi Master: "So you want a *venti* decaf breve latte?"

Me: "Yes. Thank you."

Now that I know the proper Starbuckian terminology, I can order a venti decaf breve latte wherever I go. Nowadays I usually ask for a shot of sugar-free vanilla as well.

Ordering a Starbucks beverage is kind of like doing evangelism today—both are an adventure that requires learning and listening, patience and perception, daring and decisiveness. We embark on the adventure of evangelism when we enter into a relationship with Jesus, and throughout the journey God molds and matures us. I've written this book because I believe the adventure of evangelism is the best way to grow in faith and maturity in Christ. I want to help empower you to be an effective witness, but I also want you to experience the lasting joy and freedom that come with the adventure.

The more time we spend with lost people, the more we become like Christ. Contradictory as it may seem, we encounter God in the treasure hunt for lost hearts more tangibly than we ever could in a worship service, small-group Bible study or prayer gathering. The adventure requires us to listen patiently for the voice of the Holy Spirit. It requires us to learn a new language in order to engage our world. It requires us to connect with those to whom we've been sent. The adventure also demands that we become perceptive about our culture, take risks, and develop faith, decisiveness and boldness. However, the adventure also requires love and grace, mercy and caring. It is an adventure with many paradoxical twists and turns, but along the way we get to peer into the heart of God and learn what it really means to be his witnesses.

The adventure for the lost is also a lost adventure. Few Christians today understand what a privilege they have in being invited to participate in Jesus' effort to seek and save the lost. It's like a father who asks his son to join him for a summer workday. The sweat of their labor gives their relationship an additional dimension. If the father explained the work and its value but never asked his son to join him, the son would grow up with a skewed view of work, the world and his place in it. Jesus invites us, even begs us for our own benefit, to run alongside him as he seeks the lost.

I've been doing evangelism since December 25, 1989, which is the day I became a Christian at the age of twenty. Much of what I've learned over the years has been through trial and error—mostly error, so go ahead and laugh at my mistakes. I hope you will also learn from my corrected successes. Seldom in this book will you encounter theory and rhetoric; rather, the lessons I wish to share are found in the stories of my own adventure. I invite you to watch for the instruction in the narrative and ask yourself how it applies in your own life. An application section at the end of each chapter will help you do this.

There are two sections to this book. The first deals with being the kind of person God wants us to be and explores how the adventure of evangelism helps us become that person. The second section examines the kinds of people God wants us to reach out to. Parents and relatives, strangers and colleagues, friends and neighbors—there are many types of people in your adventure, and I've tried to provide lots of examples of how to reach out to them—and how not to.

In each chapter, I'll introduce you to someone I've met in my own adventure and ask you to "tag along" with me in the story. I hope to give you many glimpses of what an evangelistic encounter looks like and show what God can do through these experiences. Your stories will inevitably differ from mine; in fact, I hope you avoid many of my mistakes. But I trust you will see that God works through everyday Christians to bring lost people to faith and that the adventure is not merely for the "professionals." I hope my stories are helpful and encouraging as you seek to share Jesus with the people in your life.

Also in each chapter, you will notice statements in the margins labeled "Uncommon Sense." These statements are universal principles that must find their way into both our character and our practice if we are to witness effectively. I refer to them as "uncommon" because God's wisdom is just that—uncommon. God's perspective is often paradoxical to us and unless we think outside the box, we will miss it. The statements often encapsulate what I learned from my encounter with the person I'm describing. You may want to record your own observations and examples in the margins alongside the "Uncommon Sense" entries.

For more information about InterVarsity Christian Fellowship, visit <www.intervarsity.org>.

Who am I to write such a book? I am an adventurer! I love the adventure for what it does in the lives of those around me and for what it has done for my own character. I love evangelism even though it is the scariest and most exhausting aspect of my Christian faith. I am the director for regional evangelism in the Great Lakes region for InterVarsity Christian Fellowship, an international evangelism movement on college campuses.

I have been doing evangelism professionally for some years, but it is as risky and radical for me now as it was in my first few days as a Christian. Evangelism doesn't become easier or less adventuresome as we do it more, but we can become freer and more fruitful if we take the adventure seriously. It is a work that will grow and stretch every Christian who undertakes it. I am thankful that I've allowed God to use the adventure in my life, and I encourage you to let God use it in yours as well.

Because the adventure of evangelism is largely becoming lost, many words that I use might seem unusual, outdated or unfamiliar to some readers. For this reason, let me briefly comment on a couple of these words. Of first importance is the word *evangelism* itself. Evangelism is the process of intentionally and verbally sharing the good news about the life, death, resurrection and loving leadership of Jesus with those who do not have a relationship with God. The work of evangelism revolves around the message that Christians for two thousand years have referred to as "the gospel," and it does not happen by accident. Most importantly, evangelism is the duty and privilege of every Christian.

Second, the Bible teaches that there are two kinds of people in our world, lost people and found people, and God and all his found people are in a hunt for all the lost people. I use the term *lost* to refer to anyone who has not entered into a relationship with God through Jesus Christ. I do not mean to conjure up echoes of ultrafundamentalistic preaching or images of cartoon figures melting in a lake of fire, I assure you. But I do want to emphasize that people are lost and in peril and because of this, the adventure is an urgent rescue mission.

One final issue before you venture into the content of this book: each of the stories in these thirteen chapters is absolutely true. However, some names and identifying details have been altered to protect the privacy of the people being described. Now, having said all that, enjoy this book of stories and may God bless you in your own adventure!

PART ONE

Being God's Witnesses

1

UNDERSTANDING THE GOSPEL

It was an exciting time to be alive. The snow was melting off rooftops, tulips were beginning to pierce the frost-packed earth, and I was a bounding new Christian. My senses seemed to wake up for the first time ever—the spring air had never smelled so sweet, the sky never looked so ice-blue as it did that March of 1990. I walked around the University of Michigan in Dearborn with a smile plastered to my face and a large, leather-bound Bible under my arm. I couldn't believe what a difference following Christ had made on my life in just three months and I couldn't stop talking about it. I quickly learned that one of the greatest secrets to the Christian faith is that by giving our faith away to others, we grow in joy, maturity and satisfaction with God.

I became addicted to speaking about Jesus not only for what I saw it do in the life of others but also for what it did in my own life. I had entered an adventure with Jesus himself—the adventure of spreading the good news of forgiveness. I shared my faith with my fraternity brothers, my family and friends, my college professors, strangers on the street—anyone I came across with a pulse and a working set of ears. I experienced what people call being "born again."

At the same time, however, I became acutely aware of just how much I needed to grow in order to become an effective witness for

Jesus. I had no lack of energy or motivation, but I needed to increase in my ability to spread the good news. So I read incessantly. I read Josh McDowell's *Evidence That Demands a Verdict* cover to cover. I read Francis Schaeffer's complete works. I read Jonathan Edwards, Billy Graham, Dietrich Bonhoeffer, J. I. Packer, John Wesley, Martin Luther, John Calvin, Charles Finney, D. L. Moody and Charles Spurgeon. I read books on apologetics, theology, archaeology, evangelism, Christian living and biblical hermeneutics.

Above all, however, I was drawn to the study of eschatology. I attended seminars and conferences on prophecy and read as much as I could about the end times. The fact that my newfound Savior was literally going to return to earth floored me like no other truth I had heard. I couldn't figure out why my new Christian friends were so blasé about it. It was all I wanted to talk about and all I could think about as I lay awake on my bed night after night. I also believed there was no greater reason for lost people to give their lives to Christ, so I frequently spoke about it with my classmates and coworkers.

UNCOMMON SENSE

The best way to grow our faith is to give it away.

At the time I was working in the campus library's audiovisual department with a guy named Chris. I spent many a night with Chris locking down the campus buildings and storage closets—a job that took hours. As we went from building to building, I poured out my newly acquired knowledge in no particular order and with very little explanation.

"Chris, let me explain what the Bible says about Daniel's seventy weeks of years!"

"Chris, do you realize that when Jesus comes back, he will return to the Mount of Olives in Israel?"

"Chris, let me tell you about the mark of the beast in Revelation 13:18!"

Looking back, it's a wonder I didn't scare the living daylights out of Chris. But he rarely challenged what I was saying and seemed genuinely interested. We also discussed evolution, philosophic proofs for God's existence, archaeological discoveries and how Christ was changing my life. I must have come off as an unmanned fire hose, flailing and bursting with information with no sign of letting up. Chris would typically listen quietly and nod a little. When I paused between spurts, he occasionally repeated what I had said to reassure me that he was listening.

After several weeks of inundating Chris this way, I stopped one day before work at a picnic table thawing in the midafternoon sun. "Why hasn't Chris become a Christian yet, Lord?" I prayed.

Let us ask ourselves the question, "Is love the motivating power that urges us to go out and work for God?" This is the first question that we ought to ask ourselves.

D. L. MOODY

"I've told him everything I can think of. It seems like he understands and agrees. God, what do I do now?"

I heard the Holy Spirit ask back, "Have you tried sharing the gospel with him?"

Well! I stood straight up, power-walked into the library early for my shift, took out my black king-sized preacher's Bible, and went to work in my concordance. I looked up the word *gospel*, thinking that this most basic Bible message would be easy to define for Chris with one or two passages. The more I read, however, the more confused I became. What exactly *was* the gospel, anyway? Chris came in and found me sweating over my Bible. "Hey, York. Studying away as usual, I see."

"Chris, I have to talk to you about something important," I answered.

"In fact, it's more important than all of the other things we've been talking about combined."

Chris, surprisingly, looked relieved and said, "Let's have dinner together in the staff lounge, then."

I agreed and went back to work trying to figure out what this gospel was that I was scheduled to explain to him that evening.

After many years of training others to explain the gospel, I've come to realize some important things. The gospel is the message that looses salvation. It throws open the gates of heaven and shuts the gates of hell. It converts sinners and chastens believers. The gospel is the very heartbeat of the Christian life, and there is no more glorious aspect of our faith. Without the gospel message, there is no Christianity, no salvation, no relationship with God, no kingdom of heaven, no freedom from death and hell. The gospel is the mystical, magical message of the Messiah. It has a unique power and inherent spiritual pull that is impossible to escape yet difficult to clearly define. It possesses a mysterious and often puzzling influence that captivates its hearers despite the shortcomings of those who speak it. When uttered, this message transcends the ordinary mouthpiece from which it proceeds and launches straight into the human soul.

I have also, however, come to the following conclusion: For all its simplicity and power, the gospel is one of the most elusive and misrepresented messages of the Christian faith. We Christians are often prone to what I call "gospel amnesia," and I was a classic example before my meeting with Chris. Here I was, saved by the gospel and just hours away from presenting it, and I didn't have a clue where to begin. I scoured Scripture, but every passage containing the word *gospel* seemed to cite it without defining it. This was

---

RECOMMENDED READING

The Mark of the Christian

by Francis Schaeffer

a problem, and not just because of my upcoming appointment. How could I call myself a follower of Jesus Christ and not understand the gospel message?

For months I had read every book on the Christian faith I could get my hands on, but I had neglected the message that had saved my soul. As a result, I was not prepared to share with Chris. I locked myself in the back room and sat in tears pouring through the Scriptures. Amid broken Ducane projectors, plastic carts and dusty projectors, I turned the pages of the New Testament in search of salvation. I knew that if I couldn't get the gospel right, none of the other things mattered. My heart sank as I realized that my thinking about my newfound faith was as scattered as the piles of audiovisual equipment that littered the room.

How often do we major on the minors? We've become experts on Christian self-help, Christian schooling, Christian arbitration and Christian money management. Our shelves are stocked with the latest child-rearing manuals and anecdotal inspirational booklets. But before gaining expertise in any other area of life, we must first master the most basic of all messages—the gospel of Jesus Christ. A red neon sign should go off in our spirits at the first hint of ambiguity over the gospel. Spreading its message is, after all, the first mission of every Christian.

OF FIRST IMPORTANCE

After some time in the AV room scrambling through Scripture, I finally came across 1 Corinthians 15:1-4, where Paul gives the briefest summary of the gospel we find in the Bible. Paul states that Christ died for our sin and was buried, and that he was raised from the dead on the third day. Now, this summary statement assumes that we understand a number of things. For example, what is sin? Which Jesus are we talking about? What did his death accomplish? Why is the resurrection important? How do we respond to what he has done? The Scriptures provide layer upon layer of meaning regarding Christ's death and resurrection—

justification, substitutionary atonement, regeneration, rebirth, redemption, adoption, triumph over evil, forgiveness—but it is here in this brief summary statement that we find the heart of the gospel message.

As I read the words, it was as if light broke forth and streamed off the page into that dingy room. I felt I had struck gold. I knew that Christ had died on the cross to save us from God's wrath and that through his shed blood there was forgiveness of sin. I knew that Jesus was the righteous Son of God who could not be bound by death and hell but who rose in victory over sin, death and the devil to bring us back into fellowship with the Father. I was on my way to formulating a clear gospel presentation not only for Chris, but for myself.

Six o'clock finally arrived and Chris came to get me. I looked and felt haggard from the daylong ordeal, but I was ready. I rose to my feet, tucked my Bible under my arm and led the way to the staff lounge. When we got to the empty lounge, Chris sat in an upholstered chair with an eager expression on his face. I couldn't have asked for a better situation. I had shared and defended my faith with dozens of people in the previous three or four months, but I had never proclaimed the gospel until that evening. "Chris," I began, "I'm just going to talk for a while and after I'm done, I have a question for you. Is that all right?" Chris agreed, leaning forward as I opened my Bible.

"Chris," I started, "The first thing we need to understand about God is that he loves us deeply, but there's a problem."

As I began sharing the gospel, something amazing happened. I felt a power and divine pleasure deep in my spirit that I had not sensed in any other conversation. I knew the Holy Spirit was working as I preached not only to Chris but to myself. The experience emblazoned my soul like nothing had since my salvation. I underwent another conversion in that staff lounge—a conversion to gospel proclamation.

"We're all infected with a spiritual disease called sin," I continued, "a sickness of the soul that affects every aspect of life. We know we have this disease because we rebel against God. Think about the bad things we do—lust, gossip, cheat, lie—these are the symptoms of a sickness that if left unchecked would ruin us, the people around us and even our world."

Chris said he understood, and I continued, "The sad fact is that we love rebelling against God's ways and we choose to go our own way. Eventually, by continuing to follow the desires of the disease of sin, we find ourselves forever separated from God. The Bible tells us in Hebrews 9:27 that we are all going to die and after we do, we will face God to be judged. Because of our sin and the path we have chosen, we will fall short of God's standard of perfection. God is perfect, he is holy, he is without sin. Even if God wanted to forgive us, he must judge us because he is holy and we are sinners.

I asked Chris whether all this made sense, giving both him and myself a chance to catch our breath and to make sure I wasn't leaving him in the dust. Again, he said that it made sense so far, so I went on: "If we die without our sin disease cured or our bad things paid for, we will be eternally separated from God in a place called hell. Hell is where we suffer the punishment for our misdeeds without any hope of parole.

"This sounds like a bad dilemma, but remember that God loves us deeply. He doesn't want people to follow their own way toward destruction. He doesn't look forward to sending anyone to hell. So he did something about our situation. He sent Jesus to earth. Because Jesus was God's Son, he was sinless. He never broke God's laws and did what none of us could possibly do—live a sinless life.

"Do you know any perfect people, Chris?" I asked.

"No," he answered. "Nobody's perfect."

"Nobody except Jesus, and that's important," I added. "I'm sure you've heard that Jesus died on the cross. Well, because Jesus was perfect, his death on the cross accomplished two very important things. First, the blood he shed is God's antibiotic for our sin disease. Through applying the blood of Jesus to our souls, God can begin to reverse the stranglehold of sin. Second, when Jesus suffered on the cross, he took the full punishment of our sin upon himself. The Bible says in Isaiah 53 that Jesus was pierced for our transgressions, or misdeeds.

"Finally, Jesus didn't stay dead. On the third day he came back to life, proving that he could pay for all of our sins and beat death and hell. Jesus said that by believing in him, we can also beat death and be raised again. Every believer in Jesus has the hope of heaven—the certainty that when we die we won't stay dead but, like our leader, we will come to life again through his power.

"Because Jesus is alive, we can know him today. It is knowing Jesus and following him on a daily basis that allows us to live life the way it was intended—abundantly, fully and freely. I know this is a lot to take in, but are you with me so far?" I asked.

"Yes, go on," Chris said.

"The last part of the message has to do with how we respond. The Bible tells us we must repent if we are to receive the gift of Jesus. Repent means to recognize or to reconsider. We recognize our sin disease, we recognize our misdeeds, we recognize the path we're on and we reconsider what to do about our situation. When we repent, we basically say to God that we want his way and we are willing and ready to turn over our lives to his leadership. We acknowledge our sin, ask God for his forgiveness and power and decide to follow Jesus as our Lord. When we repent, we place our full trust in what Jesus has done for us, not what we can do for God. We trust in his complete and satisfactory death and resurrection and ask him to save us from sin's consequences. So my question to you, Chris, is this: Are you ready to give control over to God and admit your sin? Do you want to become a follower of Jesus—a Christian?"

I looked up at Chris. He was smiling at me from his oversized chair. "I wondered when you would get around to this, York," he said. "For these past few months, I've noticed a difference in you. You've been like a completely different person. But when you shared all that interesting stuff in our conversations, I never knew what the main point was. You would just talk and talk and it was all great, but I didn't know how it related to me. Now I see," he said. "This message makes sense. Of course I want to become a Christian."

I couldn't believe my ears. No debate? No challenge or question or resistance? He was going to become a Christian just like that after a twenty-minute gospel presentation? How could this be? And there it was, the most important epiphany I have ever received since becoming Christian. The gospel saves.

My changed life didn't save Chris that day. In fact, in heaven there won't be one person who's there because they observed someone else's good, moral Christian life. To be sure, Christian charity, personal piety and the pursuit of social justice must go hand in hand with gospel proclamation. But we must never believe our behavior to be a substitute. Being good and doing good can't do anything more than predispose someone to listen to and appreciate the Christian faith. No, we must always also proclaim the gospel, for it is the power of God for salvation.

My knowledge of various prophetic subjects and my ability to offer apologetic reasoning didn't save Chris that day either. While Chris did, surprisingly, find my bombastic musings interesting, he didn't really understand much of what I shared with him. In the end they were nothing more than esoteric

UNCOMMON SENSE

By majoring on the minors and not being clear on the gospel, we confuse people and make it more difficult for them to come to Jesus. By majoring on the message of the gospel, we open the gates of heaven and invite them to follow the living Jesus.

ramblings that confused Chris more than anything. I don't want to imply that talking to people about evidences for faith or other aspects of the Christian life are always without fruit. Our conversations did seem to create a hunger in Chris. Unfortunately, like many Christians, I talked around the gospel and never quite made it to the heart of the matter, producing a hunger without offering the food that could satisfy it.

No, that evening it was Jesus who saved Chris, and he did it through the gospel message. I explained it as simply as I've ever done—no props or diagrams or stories or illustrations. All I had was my big black preacher's Bible and a newfound understanding of the core of the Christian message. Oh, what power and pleasure there is in this simple utterance! What secret joy is to be had merely by speaking it!

SHARING THE PLATFORM WITH BILLY GRAHAM

One of my biggest heroes is Billy Graham. I look up to him primarily for one reason: he has preached the gospel in its simplicity for more than fifty years. I have listened to recordings of sermons he delivered on the streets of Los Angeles in 1949. I have listened to sermons he preached in the twilight of his life despite frailty and life-threatening sickness. And what I have found over the course of a lifetime of ministry is his commitment to proclaim the simple gospel message and invite people to respond.

I often hear Christians try to excuse themselves from evangelism by saying, "Well, I'm no Billy Graham." That evening with Chris I shared a platform with Billy Graham because I preached Christ in simplicity, in power and with the anointing of the Holy Spirit. The exciting truth of evangelism is that by keeping to the gospel message, every believer can stand with Billy Graham on God's stage of history and be proclaimers of the powerful message of Jesus. We might not ever achieve worldwide influence or notoriety, but we can all be God's evangelists. In fact, we must!

I led Chris in a mangled sinner's prayer. After we prayed he asked, "So now what?" I responded, "Now, Chris, your new life begins!" I was so excited that I gave him my own Bible until I could buy him one. We agreed to meet twice a week to study the Word and pray. Chris transferred to an out-of-state college just months after giving his life to Christ, but in those short months I watched Jesus transform his life, just as he had mine.

Chris read his Bible at work, got involved in a good church, prayed regularly and even began sharing his faith. As I watched this happen, I became persuaded of the importance of discipleship. The Lord had doubled my evangelistic efforts at my job by saving Chris—now there were two of us proclaiming the gospel. Since this experience, my desire has been to see new believers begin to grow immediately, and the central aspect of their growth involves learning to proclaim Jesus early on. In fact, I assert that new Christians who immediately learn to evangelize grow faster, are better rounded, experience more joy and success, and are generally more thankful than those who do not. It is, after all, the mission and identity of God's people to be his witnesses on earth until he returns.

APPLICATION

Too often we fumble around in our relationships with lost people, never really getting to the heart of the matter. We talk around Jesus without introducing people to him. There are many reasons why this happens. Sometimes we are fearful. Other times we lack faith in God or the power of the gospel. Still other times we're afflicted with gospel amnesia. But as far as I can see, reaching lost people is one of the only things we can do this side of heaven that we won't be able to do when we're with the Lord. What holds us back?

A lack of knowledge produces fear and apprehension. I've learned this to be true in all sorts of things: investing money, going on a trip, starting a business, writing a book. But in all these undertakings, my fear has dissipated as I obtained knowledge. Proclaiming Christ is no different. Our irrational fears and apprehension will diminish in direct proportion to our knowledge of the gospel and its power. Acquiring training, reading books, studying the Bible and actually practicing evangelism will increase our boldness. In the end, however, freedom in evangelism comes from being convinced that the gospel saves and that from its message emanates a supernatural power to transform lives.

Are you like I was before I met with Chris—a bit fuzzy on the details of the gospel and unsure how to teach it to others? If so, let me challenge you to reread my dialogue with Chris, making notes on the gospel elements. You might want to jot down additional Scripture passages that come to mind. Let me also challenge you to share the gospel message with someone near you. If you're sitting with friends who don't have a relationship with Jesus, perhaps you could put this book down and say something like, "I was just reading this book and it made me want to stop and ask you some questions." Or, "Have you ever heard the most basic message of the Christian religion before?" Regardless of how you start or with whom you start, the point is to start. Without beginning our own personal journey of gospel proclamation, we will never reach the countless masses. Why not start today by sharing with just one person?

UNCOMMON SENSE

Freedom in evangelism comes from the realization that the gospel saves. As we increasingly share out of a place of trust and belief in the message, we will experience the pleasure and power of God in a greater fashion.

Perhaps you are more like Chris in this story. Before we share Jesus with others, we need to know him ourselves. Do you know the good news about Jesus? More importantly, have you applied it to your own spiritual situation? Have you heard a lot about Jesus and Christianity but never actually repented of your sin and asked Christ to be your Lord? If so, I invite you to do that right now. Becoming a Christian is a matter of receiving the

RECOMMENDED READING

Believing God **by Beth Moore**

free gift of salvation, and you can do this right now. Below is a suggested prayer, which I would ask you to read out loud. The words aren't magic; the key is whether you are sincere in acknowledging your sin and in your desire to receive Christ's leadership. If you've never done this before, take the first step into the abundant life that God has planned for you.

> Dear Jesus, I know that I have the sin sickness and that I've done wrong. I'm sorry for my sins. Please, have mercy on me and forgive me. I believe that you died for my sin on the cross and that you beat death by rising from the dead. Come and take control of every aspect of my life and teach me how to be your witness. Thank you for your free gift of salvation. Amen.

If you've just prayed that prayer for the first time, let me be the first to welcome you to the family of God! I encourage you to share your decision with another Christian and to begin looking for a local church where you can grow and serve. I also urge you to begin praying and reading the Bible daily; God will teach you to follow him and experience the abundant life through these daily practices. Finally, I challenge you to share this same message with another person who does not know yet. Remember, the best way to grow your faith is to give it away. I think as you read the remainder of this book, you will find more illustrations to guide you in sharing with those around you.

2

PARTNERING WITH GOD

'll have to call you back, honey, my cell phone is losing reception," I said as I wound through the foothills of Pennsylvania. I was sad to end my conversation with my wife but deeply moved by the sight of the rocky, wintry hills rolling before me. I had a deep sense of the Lord's presence.

"God, I don't know what you have for me this weekend, but I'm going to give you my all. I'm thankful for this opportunity." As I prayed I came upon a hillside of spotted sheep that speckled the landscape. They were huddled into a mass as the winter wind whipped over their woolly coats. It was beginning to snow. Eventually I turned onto the muddy one-lane road leading to the conference center where I was to speak that weekend, my car occasionally scraping the uneven surface.

The conference was at an old camp. After checking in I made my way to my room and sat down on a rickety bed next to several handmade bunks clustered around a bathroom with no doors. There was no bedding. I hadn't brought a pillow, a sleeping bag or even a sheet, and I was beginning to get nervous. I prayed and asked God not to let me be distracted by the physical amenities of the camp—or lack thereof—but to use me the way he intended.

Many everyday encounters can throw us for a loop: a business trip where the housing isn't up to our standards, a dinner outing with neighbors and their undisciplined children, a vacation with in-laws where we have to quietly abide by another set of rules. In many circumstances we find ourselves challenged, pushed, squeezed and put out, and unless we ask for the "God view," we will miss the opportunity to bless others and in turn miss the blessing God has for us.

UNCOMMON SENSE

Evangelism is an adventure with Jesus where we join him in caring for his lost sheep.

As I looked out the window of my room, snow was beginning to fall in chunky clusters onto the muddy road that led to the auditorium. The conference delegates were arriving, emerging from their cars and making their way to their cabins. They reminded me of the huddled, spotty sheep on the side of the hill where I pledged to give God my all that weekend. I prayed again, "Grow my faith as you use me, Lord."

I took a walk through the woods before the first session to pray, clear my head and try to get the God view on the weekend. I knew I was to speak, but I had no idea how God specifically wanted to use me, so I was thankful for the chance to take a long walk with Jesus. The sheep came into my mind again, and I sensed the Lord saying, "Care for my sheep this weekend. My sheep will hear my voice if you allow me to speak through you." What an adventure! I felt like I was on a secret mission with Jesus, caring for his sheep and being his mouthpiece.

As I returned to my room, the sun went down and the woods became pitch black. There were no outside lights at this retreat center, so I navigated by the light of the occasional pair of headlights that bounced down the road. I finally found my quarters and changed into my preaching clothes. I had just thirty minutes to get to the auditorium—in utter darkness. I stepped out of my cabin and groped my way down the road through the darkness. "God, help me," I said, and immediately fell through a snow crust into a foot-deep pothole full of water and muck.

No need to panic. "Maybe it's not that bad," I told myself and soldiered on to the auditorium. As I opened the door and looked down, instead of tan dress pants I saw mud-colored swirls and spatters all the way up to my knees!

I quickly ran back, making sure to avoid the pit of death, changed into clean, dry pants, and dashed back to the auditorium with just minutes to spare. Moments later I was up front preaching. Finally I started to regain some equilibrium. I was preaching out of Luke 5 on the parable of the wine and the wineskins, and I was going strong—or so I thought until I saw a man asleep in the front row with his head back and his mouth wide open. "Is he that tired?" I asked myself. No one ever slept during my sermons. "Am I bombing here?"

The longer I preached, the more annoyed I got. This man, whoever he was, needed to sit up and pay attention. I was preaching the gospel, for Pete's sake. I thundered, "If you're going to follow Christ, you can't just add him to your existing plans. You can't just tweak your life a little. Following Christ requires you to be a new wineskin—entirely and utterly new. Tonight, you have to *wake up* and realize that Christ will have your full and undivided commitment or he will have no part in your life at all!"

By the end of my sermon I was bellowing, but the man continued his slumber. In fact, his head had dropped even farther back.

As I invited the audience to make a decision for Christ, I became gentle again. I thought of the spotted lambs and God's instruction to care for his sheep. But I couldn't help trying to rouse the sleeping man one more time: "If tonight you are willing to recognize your sin and trust in Christ's death on the cross and resurrection, God can save you. The choice is yours. You can continue your *slumber*, or you can wake up, confess your sin and have your sins washed clean!"

Rip Van Winkle didn't budge. Several others, however, began to come forward to the stage to give their lives to Christ. The worship that followed had a jubilant feel as we celebrated these decisions for Christ, but I couldn't celebrate knowing that this man had slept through the gospel. If he wasn't a Christian, he had missed an opportunity to meet Jesus. If he was a Christian, he had paid a great deal of disrespect to the message of the cross. Either way, I was angry and disappointed.

I returned to my room deeply disturbed. Now, however, I had a more immediate problem. The wind was howling, it was icy cold in the drafty cabin, and I had no pillow or blanket. I didn't know what to do except lay a towel on the vinyl mattress and pull my coat over me, hoping I would fall asleep quickly. No such luck. Even though I had grown up poor and slept in abandoned homes, a van and a church basement, I had never been so cold in my life. I lay there fully clothed under my coat and with my shoes on, but I quaked in my very bones.

"God, I know I said I'd give you my all here this weekend, but this is ridiculous!" I prayed. "I'm angry, frustrated and cold. Please give me your perspective." As I lay shivering, I heard God's Holy Spirit say, "Remember the spotted lambs."

I thought about those sheep huddled on the hillside being whipped by the cold wind, and I thought about the people who had come forward that night to make first-time decisions for Christ. My anger subsided and I finally drifted off to sleep.

The next day I made a point to find the sleeping man and talk to him about Christ. I located him outside a seminar room. "Hi, my name is York Moore," I said. "I'm the guest speaker this weekend. What's your name?" The thick-haired gentleman looked up, a bit annoyed, and spoke with a thick Middle Eastern accent.

"Assalamo Alaikum!" he said, which I recognized as "the peace of God be upon you" in Arabic. I answered, "Alaikum Assalam," which means "the peace of God be upon you as well."

I had studied at the University of Michigan in Dearborn, which has a large Middle Eastern population, so I had become acquainted with Islam and this greeting. "You are Muslim?" I asked. His look of annoyance changed to one of curiosity and he responded, "Yes, my friend. My name is Muhammad."

I was surprised to find an Arab-speaking Muslim at a Christian conference in the foothills of Pennsylvania, and I told him so. He explained, "I'm here because my cousin, Abidah, is interested in finding out more about Jesus, blessings be upon him. She has made many friends who are Christian and they wanted her to come to this retreat. I am here to make sure that she is safe and that she does not convert."

I glanced into the room behind us and saw a young, vibrant woman in a veil reading a Bible with another woman. In Muhammad's thinking, it was all right for his cousin to be curious about Jesus as long as at the end of the conference, she still believed him to be merely a prophet. Muhammad was keeping watch to ensure just that. "Do you have any interest in learning more about Jesus yourself?" I asked.

Sharing our faith with Muslims does not necessarily require us to become experts on Islam or to read the entire Qur'an. However, learning something about one of the fastest-growing and most influential religions in history would be wise and serve us well in sharing Jesus.

"We Muslims believe that Jesus, blessings be upon him, was a great prophet," he answered. "We honor him more than Christians do. We revere him as a great man. But we don't understand why you think he is Allah's son or why you worship him. We don't worship people in Islam, we worship Allah, the Almighty."

I responded, "I understand what you're saying. I've spoken to many imams (Islamic clergy) and have attended mosques. I've even tried my best to read the Qur'an. But I think you may have a fundamental misunderstanding of what Christians think about Jesus. We believe Jesus has always existed as a member of the Trinity, or Godhead."

Now, before I go on, let me point out that I don't believe conversations with non-Christians should typically begin with discussions of the Trinity or Christ's deity. In fact, I think we should avoid those subjects at first. However, because I knew of Muslims' love for fervent debate surrounding central issues, I felt liberty to challenge Muhammad in these areas.

I continued, "We don't believe in a three-headed god or three gods, but in one God eternally existing in three persons. Each member of the Trinity has a distinct intellect, emotion and will. Christians believe that the Trinity consists of the Fa-

RECOMMENDED READING

***Cross and Crescent: Responding to the Challenge of Islam* by Colin Chapman**

ther, the first member of the Trinity; Jesus or the Word of God, the second member; and the Holy Spirit, the third member. Does this make sense to you, Muhammad?"

He stood up and spoke with great passion. "This is what I can never accept! We believe that Allah is one and that he is alone. He does not need anyone. We don't have to create a god that needs anyone as you do."

I took a deep breath and said, "I think your concept of God is inadequate, Muhammad."

He looked surprised at the boldness of my comment. I continued, "We both agree that there is only one God. We both believe this God is inherently loving and compassionate, and that both the Bible and the Qur'an present love as having a giver and a recipient, right?"

He nodded. I went on, "We also believe that God is the only being that exists in and of himself—that is to say, he is the only one without a beginning. We both believe that God does not change; he is today what he has always been and will always be, right?"

Muhammad nodded suspiciously and stepped away a bit from the door to his cousin Abidah's seminar. "Here, then, is a problem with Islam," I said. "Who did God love before anyone existed to receive his love? Did he change to become loving? Did he create out of necessity? In Islam, Allah's aloneness is not a strength but a great weakness. Allah either depends on other beings to be who he is, or he changes in definition. Christians don't have a problem here because we say that before angels or mankind or anything else was created, love existed between the Father and the Son, between the Son and Spirit—there was a community of love. Our belief in the Trinity is not a flaw or weakness of our faith, it is our strength."

I wrapped up by saying, "We believe this community of love was the inspiration for creation. When God wanted to create a being in his image, he didn't create just a male, Adam, or just a female, Eve. He created both male and female—a community of love because he himself is a community of love. But the one thing I hope you understand from my comments is that God loves you personally, Muhammad. I know that's very different from what you've been taught in your religion."

Muhammad was silent a moment, then said, "You are very strong in your thinking. I will have to consider what you have said. Will you be here at this conference later?"

"Since I'm the main speaker this weekend, I certainly hope so!" I answered. "I'll be preaching two more times. Listen to what I say tonight and consider it. Hopefully we can speak again before the weekend is through."

Muhammad, sitting back down and looking in on his cousin, said, "I would like that very much. God bless you, my friend."

I walked away both excited and heavy in spirit. I was elated that Muhammad and Abidah were attending this conference and that I had two more opportunities to preach to them. I was also thankful for how the conversation had gone. I'd learned over the years that Muslims value passion and clarity in communication, and I had tried to achieve both in my encounter with Muhammad. He had responded well and appeared interested. However, Muhammad was a gatekeeper for Abidah to keep her out of a relationship with Jesus. What would be the consequence if she did "convert"? How would he respond?

I spent the rest of the afternoon praying while sitting in my car with the heater on. Through my windshield I saw Abidah walking with some other women. Her coat was wide open despite the cold. She was carrying a cup of hot chocolate and laughing and talking the way a child does when she's had too much sugar. Close behind her was Muhammad, jacket zipped to his chin and hands clutched behind his back. He was a good distance from the women but leaned slightly forward so he could listen.

"God, work in Abidah's life tonight," I prayed. "Please use the message to help set her free to worship you." I knew that God alone could break through to Abidah through the obstacle of Muhammad. His desire was to do so through me and the friends who had befriended and invited her.

UNCOMMON SENSE

When confronted with obstacles or difficulty, lean on God in prayer and press forward, trusting in his power.

THE POWER OF THE RESURRECTED CHRIST

The evening came and I made my way to the auditorium, this time walking way around the pit of sludge. As I stood to take the podium, I had an overwhelming sense of God's power, so I began my message by saying, "I want you to know that this evening God is going to do something miraculous."

I glanced around the auditorium for Abidah and Muhammad. I spotted Abidah's silver headscarf on the right side about halfway back. She was sitting up and paying full attention. But Muhammad was again leaning back in the front row, arms crossed and eyes closed! I shot up another prayer: "God, speak to him somehow tonight." However, just like the previous night, the longer the evening went on, the more obvious was his repose. He looked so peaceful sleeping with his mouth wide open that I began to wonder if he was faking. I ended my sermon by inviting people forward for prayer.

As I was standing in the front, praying for the many who had come forward, I noticed Muhammad in the corner of my eye. He was standing at the foot of the stage about a foot from the worship band, and his mouth was moving to the words of the song: "I worship you, Jesus. I worship you, Jesus."

I bolted through the crowd, yelling, "Muhammad. Come here!" His face was red and puffy as he shouldered his way toward me. "What has happened to you, my friend?"

"I was asleep during your message," he answered. No! Really? "As I slept, a man in white came to me in a dream and said, 'Muhammad! Get up. Go to where the man is speaking and worship me, Jesus!'" A huge smile spread across his face and he exclaimed, "That is what I did! I am here, worshiping Jesus! Tonight I find my God, Jesus!"

I could not believe my ears. For years I had heard stories of Jesus appearing in dreams to Muslims, particularly in the Middle East, but I had never in my wildest dreams thought I would witness such a conversion.

I responded, "Muhammad, that's wonderful! I would like to pray with you to recognize your commitment to worship and follow Jesus, if that's all right with you." He agreed and I led him in prayer for forgiveness of sins and belief in Christ's death and resurrection. As Muhammad continued singing with the crowd, I looked back and saw Abidah. She was weeping and jumping up and down. As I made my way back to her, the women who had befriended her were hugging her with enormous smiles on their faces.

"Abidah," I said, "what are you doing?"

Still jumping up and down, she exclaimed, "I am worshiping Jesus! I am worshiping Jesus! I am so happy." I hugged her and jumped up and down too for a moment before praying a prayer of repentance with her as well. I walked away from the crowd, overwhelmed at what God had done.

As I sat in the back watching the crowd worship, I reflected on the experience. I was awestruck by God's power. "God," I said, "You are so real!" I began to sob as I continued, "I am so thankful that I get the blessing of joining you in this adventure. I am so thankful that you are alive and that you still speak. Thank you for appearing to Muhammad tonight. Thank you for removing Abidah's gatekeeper and better yet transforming him into a worshiper! I worship you too tonight."

God not only broke into the conference and into the hearts of Muhammad and Abidah, he also broke into my heart that night. Here is the great mystery and profound blessing of evangelism: God is the evangelist who invites us into his work. As we join him in the adventure, we are always changed, always transformed, always challenged.

Dreams are very important to Muslims; many of them believe God speaks directly to people while they sleep. Christian missionaries working with Muslims have found that helping Muslims understand how God may be speaking to them personally through dreams has been a persuasive tool in the work of evangelism.

Evangelism is ultimately God's doing. He invites us into his work of reaching people, and we must learn to follow his lead even when it doesn't make much sense. Jesus is the great evangelist who seeks his lost spotted sheep. As his partners in the adventure, we get the unspeakable privilege of being his hands, mouth and voice. In the end, however, Jesus is the one who saves.

This partnership with Jesus transforms us. One of the saddest realities of Western Christianity is that the vast majority of believers fail to lay claim to this privilege. Few Christians share their faith and fewer still experience the life-changing joy of seeing men and women come to worship Jesus. Evangelism is by design a work that takes place when we in partnership with Jesus make known his death and resurrection. That night, as I stood proclaiming this eternal truth, Jesus did the work of etching himself onto the souls of two Muslims, even as one slept!

You may never be a conference speaker or an evangelistic preacher, but God wants to use you in the lives of countless people, many on a daily basis. In fact, the vast majority of people who become Christians do so through the ministry of friends, not evangelistic preachers. God uses ordinary, everyday people in ordinary, everyday situations. The great news is that God never calls us to stand alone as we speak about him but always stands with us, working in and through us. God never prompts us to step out in faith and share Christ without simultaneously working in the soil of the heart to which we are witnessing. He meets us more than halfway. Even when it seems like a person's defenses are up and the situation is hopeless, the resurrected Christ can still break through.

UNCOMMON SENSE

Jesus is the great evangelist who invites us to join him in his work of reaching the lost.

APPLICATION

Be open to God. This might seem like a simple, even trite application, but it is one of the most challenging of life's lessons. People often ask me how they can know God's will. I usually respond that it's not knowing God's will that's difficult, it's accepting and obeying God when he speaks. When God speaks and we hear him, then we are obliged to obey. It might seem scary, but giving up control and looking for the God view is the most fulfilling way to live. It is also God's method of transforming us and allowing us to experience him personally.

RECOMMENDED READING

SoulTsunami **by Leonard Sweet**

Hearing and responding to God's voice is an adventure—scary, risky and sometimes uncomfortable. But it is on this adventure that our lives are transformed and we get to witness God at work. Place this book aside and spend some time in listening prayer. Bring to mind people in your life who don't know Jesus, people who are difficult to work with, people who annoy or challenge you. Think about people who belittle or even persecute you. Think about the challenges that these people present. Now, clear your mind and ask God to tell you what to do about these difficult people.

As you listen, be open to hearing some risky answers. God is a God of surprises. His thoughts are not our thoughts, the Scriptures tell us. Don't limit him or box him in. Allow God to be God and to lead your life.

After you're done praying and listening, try to take one step in acting on what you've sensed from God. If you didn't sense anything, don't give up but keep practicing listening prayer throughout your day. I often pray and listen for God's voice without hearing anything. So I go about my day, only to hear him speak at another, often surprising time. Above all, know that God is the God of the possible. If we learn anything from the story of Muhammad and Abidah, it is that God can make a way even when there seems to be no way.

3

FOLLOWING THE HOLY SPIRIT

Trust your intuition; fate is guiding your life." I sat fumbling with the curled little fortune from the previous night's Chinese dinner trying to focus my mind for my morning quiet time. The paper was smudged with General Tso's sauce and grease from my fried rice. I laughed at how ridiculous this fortune was. How could anyone possibly take these things seriously? Intuition! What a bunch of nonsense! Intuition involved hunches and impressions without the assistance of any rational process—the last thing I would ever admit to. How could we know anything without the use of reason?

My mind danced from the greasy fortune to the birds chirping outside the window to my open Bible. I just could not focus. What was fate, anyway? I turned the scrap of paper over and over in my fingers. Nothing but a lazy person's way of throwing his hands in the air and letting some unknown source rule him. I was now mocking the disposable forecast. Finally I threw the fortune aside and got on my knees: "God, I pray that you would speak to me today." I sat down again quietly, waiting to hear from God while leafing through my Bible.

Before I began to read, however, I heard God say, "Get up, put on your Rollerblades and skate up to the main road." What a strange order! I had learned by this point in my Christian walk that when God speaks, he speaks specifically and often tells me to do things I would never come up with on my own. Still, this command was weird—and not entirely welcome. I was tired from a party the night before and looking forward to spending the day in the calm and quiet of my empty house. I didn't want to get involved in God's daily adventure of seeking lost people. But I had asked God to speak to me, and he had. I got up, went out to the garage and put on my Rollerblades.

As I skated up the street I prayed, "All right, Lord, why am I going up to the main road?" God brought an image to mind of a young man walking down the street in a winter coat. I sensed him saying, "Tell this man about me." I began to wonder if I was really hearing the Lord or if the sauce on my General Tso's chicken had muddied my brain. It was the middle of summer and already in the midseventies at ten o'clock in the morning. No one in their right mind would be walking the busy streets of Detroit with a coat on. Nevertheless, I skated on.

I rounded the corner onto Grand River Boulevard, nearly falling over as a bus whooshed by and dodging the deep cracks, holes and empty liquor bottles near the bus stops. I was nearing two major motel complexes where prostitutes worked night and day. Even at this early hour they were working the streets, flagging down passing vehicles.

I skated up the street, and in the distance I saw a young black man walking toward me in a big, puffy black ski jacket. I couldn't believe it, but there was the man the Holy Spirit had told me about. As I skated closer, I knew he was the reason I had been summoned from my home that morning. Still, when I reached the man, an overwhelming sense of fear came over me and I skated right by him. I couldn't explain it. I prayed, "Lord, give me the boldness to step out in faith." I turned around and began skating toward the man again. But again fear gripped me and I breezed right past him.

I have found over the years that when it comes to obeying the Holy Spirit, the clearer and more precise the instructions are, the more difficult they are to carry out. I used to think that if God would tell me exactly what he wanted me to do, it would be easy to do it. Not true. It's much easier to obey general, feel-good instruction from God than specific commands. In these situations we find we have to trust him even more. Fear and apprehension are also often evidences of spiritual forces of darkness at work to keep us from doing the will of God. There certainly was an element of spiritual warfare going on here.

I must have skated passed the young man five times before getting the courage up to stop and talk to him. By then, he was acting suspicious.

"Excuse me," I said. "I know this is going to sound really strange; in fact, it sounds strange to me too. But I have to tell you something. Do you have a second?"

"What is it, man?" he exploded, with obvious and extreme agitation.

I was petrified. The man was young and muscular. He was wearing a winter coat in the summer, and he could have been hiding anything in those pockets. I guessed that he was a drug dealer, pimp or young thug carrying a gun for protection.

"I know this is going to sound crazy," I began nervously, "but about thirty minutes ago, I was sitting in my living room two streets over. I was praying, when all of a sudden God told me to get up, put on my skates and go up to this road, where I would see a man walking down the street in a winter coat. When I saw you, I couldn't believe it! God has sent me to you today because he has a message for you."

I blurted it all out, and it sounded as strange to me as it must have to him. But I reasoned that since the Holy Spirit had given me this bizarre instruction, I was going to put all my cards on the table and let the chips fall where they may.

GOD SPEAKS THROUGH HIS WITNESSES

The man's face relaxed a bit. I said, "My name's York, what's yours?"

"Junior. My name's Junior and I live right over there." He pointed to

a small, rundown yellow house behind the neon-blinking motel.

"How do you deal with all the prostitutes living behind the motel?" I
asked.

Junior responded, "I moved in with
my grandmother to help protect her
from all this drama. A couple of
months ago someone tried to get in
through her kitchen window in the
middle of the night while she was
home. There's too much crime in this
neighborhood."

UNCOMMON SENSE

**We need to carefully
question the people we
speak with in order to
discern what they know
about the gospel and
proceed to share Christ
from there.**

I agreed and went on to explain
what, exactly, I thought God wanted me to say. "Junior, I believe God
wants to tell you today that he sees you, he knows you and he desires
to do good things in your life. What do you know about Jesus Christ?"

"Well, I used to go to church with my grandmother when I was a kid.
I remember that Jesus is the Son of God."

Over the years I've come to recognize this statement as the number
one answer by far when people are asked to share their knowledge about
Jesus. This confession is so eerie, yet so common, that I think we need
to watch for it. It's almost as if the Holy Spirit is communicating through
the mouths of the people we're sharing with, saying, "You found the
right one. I'm at work right here and right now in this person's life. Go
for it!"

I continued, "Do you know anything else about Jesus?"

"Just that he's the Savior of the world."

Beginning with Junior's basic understanding of Jesus, I shared the rest
of the message of salvation with him. Yes, Jesus is the Savior or the
world, but just knowing that fact doesn't make someone a Christian.

People I train in evangelism often wonder why I spend so much time explaining the gospel to churchgoing, professing Christians. It's because these are often the people who have never heard or understood the gospel. When someone tells me she is a Christian or seems to know a little about the Christian message, I usually say something like, "That's great. Do you mind if I share a couple things with you and get your impressions to see if we're on the same page?"

As I shared the gospel message with Junior, he was particularly interested to hear that believing in Jesus meant more than not going to hell. Salvation through Jesus does involve rescue from destruction, but more importantly it leads to a new and amazing life with God. "Through Christ's death and resurrection we can be forgiven of our sin and brought into a relationship with God," I explained. "God wants to save you away from death and judgment and into an ongoing, day-by-day relationship with himself. That's why I was praying and listening to God this morning about you. I have a relationship with a real God who really speaks. It isn't always an easy relationship, but following God is always an adventure."

UNCOMMON SENSE

Just because a person says he or she is a Christian doesn't mean they have heard, understood or responded to the gospel. We need to check for understanding and often share Christ anyway.

Junior gazed into the distance and began to open up. "You know, I dropped out of college last year. I was doing pretty good until I got involved with some stuff and had to leave school. Then I moved here and things got worse. I started praying and going back to church with my grandmother a couple of weeks ago because I didn't know what else to do."

I cannot tell you how often I've heard these words when talking to someone in obedience to the Holy Spirit. When God leads us to minister to particular people, it is often as part of a much larger work in their lives. Many times the person we're speaking to is already responding to God, opening up more and more to him. Then God brings us along to "seal the deal," or at least bring that person a step closer to himself.

I like to say that God never shuts up. Nineteenth-century poet Francis Thompson called him the "Hound of Heaven," meaning that God is always pursuing us with his love. In fact, without God's initiating work no one would ever respond to him; the Bible tells us that no one seeks after him on their own. There are two types of people in the world: people responding positively to God's work in their life and people responding negatively. It follows then that there will always be people who want to hear our message, like Junior, and people who do not want to hear our message. Evangelism will never be easy; it will always involve difficult tasks and stepping out in faith. But understanding these two kinds of responses and knowing we have nothing to do with them can take a lot of the weight off our shoulders and put it where it belongs—on God's.

UNCOMMON SENSE

Everyone we speak with is either responding positively to God's work in their life and moving toward him or responding negatively to God's work in their life and moving away from him. But God is always at work. He is never silent.

I finished with Junior by explaining, "I believe God has sent me here today in answer to your prayers and to bring you into a relationship with himself. It definitely sounds like you need God, and it begins when you confess your sins and believe that Jesus died for you. Christ died on the cross for your sin and he rose from the dead on the third day and because of that, Junior, you can be forgiven, cleansed and delivered from God's wrath into a relationship with him. Is that something that you want?"

It didn't take Junior more than a few seconds to respond, "Yeah. Let's do this! I want him in my life."

I prayed with Junior to receive Christ and then wrote down his contact information and thanked him for talking to me. He answered, "I should be thanking you. Thanks for listening to God today."

I skated up the road and over to my street, took off my Rollerblades and walked back into the house. As I sat down where I had prayed for God to speak to me, I noticed my curled-up greasy fortune: "Trust your intuition; fate is guiding your life." I began to think about this statement in light of the Holy Spirit's strange instruction and my time with Junior. Now, I don't believe Christians should ever look to fortune cookies for direction. But the more I thought about this fortune, the more I recognized a kernel of truth. If I were to re-state it, it would read, "Trust God today; the Holy Spirit is leading your life."

When we place ourselves before God and ask him sincerely to speak to us, he does. I wouldn't necessarily call it intuition, but discerning the Spirit's voice does in many ways transcend rational processes. We don't always hear a clear voice in our souls, but God desires to speak directly to us and lead our lives tangibly. He guides us through the principles of Scripture, yes, but he also gives us specific instructions—down to what we should put on our feet and what his lost sheep will be wearing.

Learning to hear God's voice is a process that works itself out over the course of an entire life. Much of our ability to hear God clearly is connected to whether we act in obedience when he does speak. If you have never gone through the book *Experiencing God*, I strongly recommend it as an important step in your spiritual journey. It has been one of the most influential books in my life. Going through this workbook will greatly help you to learn how to hear God, know you've heard him and follow him when he does speak.

How often do we get up, carry out our daily plans and ask God to bless what we've done? Many Christians think they can live life the way that feels best and if it's "God's will," it will all work out in the end. This is not Holy Spirit living; this is trusting intuition and hoping in fate. The Scriptures are chock-full of godly men and women to whom God gave unique and individual instruction. I believe this can be a normal part of the Christian walk. We need to know the Bible above all else;

RECOMMENDED READING

Experiencing God: Knowing and Doing the Will of God by Henry T. Blackaby and Claude V. King

trusting feelings and mental images can get us into a lot of trouble unless we're grounded in God's Word. Having said this, however, every Christian needs to ask for, wait for and expect God to direct their lives supernaturally on a regular basis. This is the normative way of relating to God, and it has been true in my life.

APPLICATION

What would have happened that day had I not bowed my head and asked God to speak to me? Even if the Holy Spirit had still prompted me about Junior, I wouldn't have been in a position to hear. What if I hadn't liked what I had heard and concluded that the Spirit's instruction was too strange, risky or costly? What if I had chickened out permanently when skating past Junior?

God is always speaking, even at this very moment. The kind of relationship he desires with his children takes place moment by moment, not hour by hour, day by day, week by week or year by year. Unfortunately, most of us—myself included many times—experience far less than a moment-by-moment relationship with the Spirit.

As you read these words, I believe God is saying something to you through the Holy Spirit. Can you hear him? What is he saying? Does it sound strange, risky or unexpected? If so, great! It's probably him and not just your imagination. God does speak to us about the normal, safe and ordinary all the time. But he also leads us down paths we never would have imagined ourselves.

RECOMMENDED READING

Daring to Draw Near

by John White

Put this book down and spend some time listening. First, ask God to speak directly to you, not in ambiguities but with simple and direct instruction. This can be a scary and awkward thing to do, but trust that the God who loves you will protect you in the process. Second, just listen. Listen for passages of Scripture, mental pictures, words, feelings and impressions. Listen for commands for change, action, repentance or forgiveness.

If you think you hear God speak, and he ultimately will, there are three ways you can be sure it's him. First, his instruction will always line up with the Bible. If it doesn't, stop listening to that voice and ask God to help you hear him more clearly. God will never contradict his Word. Now, there's no way I could have opened my Bible and tested the Holy Spirit's command to "get up, put on your Rollerblades and skate up to the main road." This leads to the second way you can be sure you're hearing the Holy Spirit—just do it! Action really is one of the best tests. In my case I would have found a man walking down the street in the middle of summer in a winter jacket or I wouldn't have.

The vast majority of times I hear and obey God's Spirit, I find exactly what he brought into my mind. Other times, however, I'm wrong entirely. When I heard something telling me to put on my skates that summer morning, the worst that could have happened was that I got a little exercise. But often there are more tangible costs associated with trying out what the Holy Spirit says, so we have to listen hard and ask God to protect us along the way. If you still have doubts or think listening for God's voice is a strange idea, I challenge you to consider the story in Acts 8 about Philip and his encounter with the Ethiopian eunuch on a desert road.

The third test is to ask what the "glory factor" is. What praise and honor could God potentially receive from your successful obedience to his instruction? When I saw a man in a winter coat and God told me to share the gospel with him, how could I go wrong? It's never a bad thing for someone to hear about Jesus. It turns out that the glory factor in Junior's salvation was quite high, but regardless of the outcome God would have been glorified by my proclaiming Jesus Christ.

Hearing the Holy Spirit takes humility, prayer and practice. It's a spiritual art form that God calls all his children to perfect over the course of our lives. Obeying the Spirit's voice is admittedly more difficult than hearing, but becoming a mature follower of Jesus requires us to do both. I'm glad to say that I hear more accurately and obey more often than I used to, but I still have a long way to go. Regardless of where you are in your journey of listening and obeying, let me again ask you to put this book down, get on your knees if you are able, and ask God to speak directly to you. Afterward, listen quietly for God's Spirit and then do all you can to obey exactly what you hear.

4

EXPLAINING THE MESSAGE

Miles and miles of cornfields stretched before me as I jostled down an old two-lane highway. Combines were at work in the fields, and the smell of drying leaves, apples and cow manure wafted in through my open car windows—it was a classic back-to-school morning. I glanced at the time. "9:40 a.m.! Where is this place?" I said. I was on a short preaching tour of schools in western Michigan and looking for the next stop. "Where can you hide twenty thousand students in the middle of all this corn?"

I had a ten o'clock appointment with a student leader for the Inter-Varsity Christian Fellowship group on campus, and I didn't want to be late. I had just become convinced I was lost when a massive complex of buildings flickered into view right in front of me like a mirage in a desert. Finally!

As I ran into the student center at 10:10, a sweet, childlike voice greeted me. "You must be York Moore." The young woman had a wholesome smile and deep blue eyes.

"And you must be Kaira," I gasped, out of breath from my dash from the parking lot. "I'm sorry I'm late." We sat for a while and talked about the campus, the InterVarsity group and the day's evangelistic events. Then Kaira said something that surprised me.

"I'm really excited to evangelize with you," she said. "I've never done anything like this before, but I believe God is going to do great things!"

Typically when I take people out to share their faith for the first time, they are anything but eager. Afraid, nauseated, faint—these are the words people usually use to describe how they're feeling.

Kaira continued, "People here need to know about Jesus badly, but I never see anyone out telling them. I've felt guilty about it, but I didn't know what to say or how to go about it." Kaira wanted to learn how to evangelize so she could help lead the whole InterVarsity group in evangelism that year.

"I agree," I responded. "God is going to do great things through us today, and I believe he's going to use this experience to begin something great on this campus through InterVarsity." We prayed and went out to the dorms.

"I want you to listen and pray as I lead us in talking to people about Jesus today. Is that all right?" I asked Kaira as we walked across campus.

"That's what I was hoping you would say."

I continued, "Think of today as a scavenger hunt. Jesus is on a search for his lost sheep and we get to join him. When you look at evangelism that way, it puts a whole different twist on things." Kaira looked excited as we approached the first dorm building.

We stepped into the air-conditioned building, and I felt tingles go up my arms and neck. We walked down the first hall, knocking on half a dozen doors without response. The next door we came to was open and I could hear two girls giggling. We knocked on the metal doorframe.

"Hi," I said. "We're from InterVarsity Christian Fellowship and wondered if you had a minute for us to ask you some questions."

"Sure! Come on in," they replied. Another student was sitting at a computer typing away, but he didn't look up or acknowledge our presence.

"I'm York and this is my friend Kaira," I began.

"I'm Sara and this is Lisa," one of the girls answered. "That dork over there is Joe. Don't mind him; he's an atheist."

Rarely had I encountered such friendly people, even in the Midwest. Kaira and I sat down. "Can you tell us about your religious backgrounds?" I asked.

Most people love to talk about themselves, and asking them questions with sincere interest helps them open up. Sara went first. "I was raised a good little Catholic girl," she said. "I went to Mass once a week, completed my catechism and was confirmed."

Lisa chimed in, "I was raised Baptist, but we usually just went to church on Christmas and Easter."

Glancing at Joe pounding away at the computer, I asked, "What about you, Joe?"

Not even looking away from the screen, he responded, "I would prefer just to listen, if that's all right."

"That's fine," I said, and continued, "Would you all say there were any spiritual milestones in your lives? Were there any significant events that you can remember?"

Again, the animated Sara began. "I don't know if this is what you're looking for, but just a couple of years ago I went to a Bible study with a friend. I never knew the Bible could be so interesting. During that time I felt a nearness to God that I had never experienced before. It was strange and scary at the same time, you know?"

At this point Joe looked up at Sara, and the clickity clack of the keyboard stopped for nearly a minute.

"What about you, Lisa?"

She looked down at the floor a moment and said, "You know, just recently I started going to the Baptist church here in town. I don't know why; I don't really like it. People aren't friendly and I can't understand the pastor. I think it may be a different kind of Baptist than my church back home."

My next question was one of the most powerful and probing questions a Christian can ask. It often generates deep thought and provocative dialogue. I asked, "Where would you say you are now with God?" Asking this question can cause people who give little thought to their spiritual life begin to wrestle with God and his place in that life.

Kaira seemed a bit befuddled and looked down while the others answered. Sara said, "I think after that Bible study, I'm more interested in God than ever. I pray every day and I try to go to Mass, but it's hard here at school."

Lisa said, "I don't know where I am now. I want to do good, you know?" She paused. "I want to be good, I mean. Sometimes I just don't know why I do the things I do. I feel guilty and ashamed all the time, and I think it's because I know I'm doing things that aren't right."

UNCOMMON SENSE

Evangelism primarily involves teaching the gospel in a culturally understandable way. The message needs to be contextualized for today and also explained according to its historical and linguistic meaning.

Again, Joe stopped and stared at us. He started to say something but caught himself mid-breath. "Joe, do you have anything to add?" I asked.

"No. I'm still just listening," he said.

After asking a couple more questions, I asked the three young people if I could explain the simple message of Jesus Christ and show them how it applied to their lives. Even though Sara and Lisa were churchgoers, I didn't assume they had ever heard or responded to the gospel. In fact, I've found that religious people are among those who need to hear the gospel most. The girls were eager and even put aside their books and notepads to listen. Joe continued at the computer, but I caught him sneaking glances at me throughout my presentation.

As I began explaining the gospel, Kaira pulled away from my side and sat with the others to watch. I borrowed a piece of Lisa's large, portrait-sized art paper and began to draw on my lap, holding up the paper periodically to explain what I was drawing. I'm a firm believer that today more than ever, teaching needs to be the foundation of our evangelism efforts. Both within the church and outside of it the rampancy of biblical illiteracy demands thorough and simple instruction.

Many aspects of the message of Jesus can be contextualized—that is, translated into words and metaphors understandable to modern people. But we need to be careful. The gospel message in its original wording contains a power and centrality that contemporary metaphors and cultural translations often miss. Law, sin, death, hell, repentance, crucifixion, resurrection, faith, righteousness, lordship—this is the vocabulary of evangelism. These words are rich in meaning, pregnant with power and churning with wonder. Because of this, we must teach people what they mean so they can understand how they apply to their lives today.

RECOMMENDED RESOURCES

1. **Nelson's Electronic Bible Reference Library**

2. **The Essential IVP Reference Collection: The Complete Electronic Bible Study Resource**

I scrawled out the words of the gospel, making sure to ask for questions along the way. At one point Sara asked, "So if we can't work to make up our wrongs, why be religious at all?"

"An excellent question," I answered. "I don't think there's any good reason to be religious."

The students stared at me, waiting for a punch line that didn't come. I pressed further. "There's no use reading your Bible, going to church or praying. All of it is useless and does nothing for your soul. You might as well stop doing it."

That got Joe's attention. He stopped typing, pulled his chair around and spoke up. "Now we're on the same page. I'm surprised to hear you say that, being a minister. Explain."

I looked at Kaira, and she folded her arms as if to say, "Yeah, buddy, explain!"

LOSING MY RELIGION

Just then a student named Gary walked in. "What's going on here?" he asked.

"My name is York and this is Kaira," I said. "We're from InterVarsity Christian Fellowship and we've just been discussing with your friends how Jesus' death on the cross and resurrection from the dead can make a real difference in their lives." I laid it on thick, hoping Gary would leave or sit down quietly.

Joe added, "Yeah, and he was just going to tell us why religion is a big waste of time." He continued, "Gary here is a Christian. Isn't that right, Gary?" Joe's question sounded more like an accusation.

Gary looked embarrassed and darted a look toward Sara. I sensed that Gary was romantically involved with Sara and didn't want to look like a hypocrite in front of Joe and Lisa. He said, "Well, my parents are Christian. I'm not so sure anymore. I've started exploring other options since I came to college."

I said, "Why don't you sit down for a minute and listen as I finish up what I was saying?" Gary agreed and joined Sara on the black futon.

I continued, "If religion could save anyone, Jesus wouldn't have had to come die on the cross in our place. The disease of sin that I explained earlier is so serious that no matter how many good things we do, we can never get better on our own. Only the blood of Jesus can cure us of our sin, cleanse us from our past and deliver us from future judgment before God. People who trust in religion to make them better people are fools."

Joe answered, "That makes a lot of sense to me. I could never understand how religion benefited anyone but the guy taking the money at the front of the church. So what was so special about Jesus that his death could do all that for us?" Joe, though he was brash and to the point, was engaged now. The self-pronounced atheist of the group became my ally in articulating the gospel, asking questions that led perfectly to a discussion of the person of Christ.

"You see," I said, "the very core of the good news that I'm talking about centers on Jesus' victory over sin, death and judgment. Early in the morning of that first Easter Sunday, Jesus Christ beat death and hell when he came back to life. Through his victory over death, we can have victory in our lives. When we follow him, he empowers us to turn away from the shameful and sinful things that previously enslaved us and embrace an amazing quality of life. The Bible calls this 'abundant living,' or life to the full."

I looked at Lisa and said, "Does this make sense to you? I know you said you wanted to be a good person and that you felt guilt and shame over the way you've lived your life so far. Do you see how Jesus' resurrection from the dead can change that?"

She was tracking and answered immediately, "Yes. I never understood that before. Why didn't someone explain it to me? I've known the message you're talking about since I've been a little girl but I have never understood it until today."

I looked at Sara and asked, "Does this make sense to you?"

She uncharacteristically paused and reflected before answering, "Yes. It makes sense now."

"What about you?" I asked Joe.

He asked back, "Well, if Jesus died to take away my sin and rose from the dead, what's left to do if I'm not supposed to be religious?"

"That's another excellent question," I responded. "Let me explain. The Bible calls us to reconsider, or repent. It calls us to realize that our life now naturally leads us away from God and toward judgment. The Bible calls us to reconsider the solution to that dilemma. Instead of trusting in our own ability to please God or figure out the answers, the Bible is clear—we must trust Christ. We must place our trust solely in the fact that Jesus' blood shed on the cross and the power of his resurrection are necessary and sufficient to turn away God's holy wrath. We then ask Jesus to lead us into a different kind of life, an abundant life, where he is the leader, or Lord. It's that simple."

Throughout the presentation, Gary was silent and twitchy. Sara, Lisa and Joe were eagerly listening and responding to Jesus for the first time, but Gary, who knew the Bible and had been raised around the things of God, was resistant and cold. He looked clammy, like he was sick or had stayed up all night. It's a harrowing thing to watch someone turning away from Jesus.

"Gary," I said, "What's your response to all this?"

He tried to look confident. "I'm making my own path right now. I've heard this message all my life and I want to check out other ways."

By the look on his face and the sound of his voice, I could tell he wanted to believe what he was saying. But he didn't.

I made one last attempt. "Gary, this message is for you—not just your parents, but for you. Jesus died for you and he loves you. Don't you understand that? Is there any reason why you wouldn't want to receive that love today?"

He sounded annoyed as he answered, "I know he loves me, and if I ever come back, I'm sure he'll forgive me."

"I wouldn't be so sure about that," I shot back.

Gary looked confused, as if he'd never contemplated that possibility. It rarely occurs to people who have been around the things of God all their lives that God's grace and pursuing love have an end. He does not extend the hand of forgiveness and friendship indefinitely. It's too late for some people, particularly those who have openly and knowingly repudiated the sacrifice of God. Hebrews 10:29 speaks strongly of the punishment one deserves for trampling on the grace of God's sacrifice on the cross. Gary and many others in the church treat God's grace with disregard, therefore throwing away the only means for their forgiveness.

I turned to the others and said, "Is there any reason why you wouldn't want to repent right now and be saved? Is there any reason why you wouldn't want to enter the abundant life of friendship with God right here?"

One by one, each shook their head no. Even Joe, the atheist, was giving his life to Jesus. I continued, "If that's your desire, I'd like to pray a brief prayer with you that simply repeats what I've explained," I said. "The prayer goes like this: 'Dear Jesus, I know that I am a sinner and deserve your judgment. I acknowledge my wrong and my need of you. I believe that you died on the cross for my sin and that you beat death and are alive right now. Come into my life and lead me away from darkness into abundant living. Be my leader. Amen.' Do you understand what that will mean for each of you?"

Again, all three answered positively. I turned to Sara. "Can I pray this prayer with you today?"

"Yes," she said.

Lisa, in tears, responded next: "Yes."

Joe, taking off his baseball cap and laying it down, said "yes" as well.

But Gary turned away.

"I think it would be appropriate for us to stand and hold hands as we pray together," I said. We stood, grasped one another's hands, and prayed out loud in the dorm room. What a wonderful experience of the power of the simple proclaimed message.

After spending another thirty minutes or so counseling these brand-new believers and gathering their contact information, Kaira and I prayed for them one last time, thanked them and left. We had spent nearly two hours in that dorm room toiling, teaching and calling these young people, who were at very different places in their spirituality. My scheduled time with Kaira was at an end. On the way back to the student center, she said softly, "You know, I really needed to hear that message today."

"I know," I answered mildly. "Whenever Christians hear the gospel, it ought to ignite our souls and call us back to a full commitment to Christ."

Once back at the student center, we spoke for another ten minutes about the experience and plans for follow-up with InterVarsity. Then Kaira, with her gentle smile and kind eyes, said goodbye.

Several months later I ran into Kaira at a training conference. She told me about the wonderful things that were happening at her school and how God had used my visit to stir the InterVarsity chapter to greater fervor in evangelism. She also told me that Sara, Lisa and Joe had been contacted by the group and received Bibles shortly after

UNCOMMON SENSE

The death, resurrection and lordship of Jesus is the very essence of the gospel.

To proclaim these truths is to open the gates of heaven to all who would hear and respond—even those we might not expect.

our encounter. Then she leaned closer and said, "I have something else to tell you. Do you remember after we walked out of the dorms how I said I needed to hear that message?"

"Yes," I said.

"Well, it was because I'd never heard it before. I've been in church my whole life, but I had never heard the gospel message before that day. I

prayed that prayer with you and the others for the first time!" Her blue
eyes were full of joy.

"I can't believe it, Kaira! That's wonderful!" I said. I was overjoyed, but
I was also a little perplexed. I had been training a student leader who was
to train her whole chapter in evangelism, and she hadn't heard the message of salvation herself. That message must stand at the center of our
outreach, or all our efforts are for nothing. Still, Kaira had heard the gospel and responded. What an adventure the scavenger hunt of evangelism
with Jesus can be.

On the last day of the conference, Kaira stood before hundreds of
other college students and told the story of our encounter as people
laughed and cheered. On a Midwestern campus hidden among the cornfields, not three but four students had turned their lives over to Jesus
that day.

APPLICATION

Thousands upon thousands of people fill our nation's churches, youth
groups and campus ministries who have never heard, understood or applied the gospel truth. Some are like Gary, hardhearted, arrogant and
moving away from God. Others are like Kaira, warm and kind but ignorant of the saving message. There are people like Lisa who come and go
on major holidays, never understanding how Jesus relates to all the other
days of the year as well. Still others, like Sara, come regularly out of a
sense of tradition and duty, believing they are earning God's good favor.
Then there are the Joes of the world, would-be followers of Christ if not
for the hypocrisy and empty answers they experience from so-called
Christians.

Where are you today? Do you know the message—not just its form
and structure, but the heart that pulses at the center of it? Do you know
Jesus Christ, the one who speaks and breathes still? What about people
around you? Do they know the gospel or do they know tradition, as-

sumptions, caricatures and hypocrisy? Are there Joes in your world? Are there Lisas or Kairas? Any Garys who are slipping away?

Spend some time asking God to peel back any layers of assumption from your beliefs about yourself and people you know. Ask him to help you focus on the simple and life-changing message of the gospel and to strip away everything in your evangelism not essential to that message. Fix your mind's eye on Jesus Christ—naked, bloody, spit hanging off his left knee, heaving on the cross on a dusty road. Ask him to help you know the power of that misty morning when the military slept around an empty cave and light blazed forth in victory.

Evangelism is about these simple truths. It is about the Master and his character and work. Jesus still speaks. His words change people's lives, even our own. We are often tempted to look beyond the cross and the empty tomb in our quest for purpose, in our attempts to reach people, in our attempts to make a difference. Let us all, once again, turn our eyes upon Jesus.

5

BREAKING THE ICE

A frost line is defined as the depth to which frost penetrates the earth. We don't usually think about this geological characteristic until something happens to bring it to our attention. Shortly after I moved into my first home, I got a lesson in the effects of the frost line. I was coming home from a weekend conference tired and ready for a long Sunday nap. As I turned the corner onto my street, however, I saw a caravan of city sewage trucks camped in front of my home with a backhoe and little blue tents. About fifteen men were looking into a deep, wide hole, and almost the entire block was covered in thick ice—lawns and landscaping included.

I parked my car in front of my neighbor's house, and Steve came out to meet me, hands jammed into his pockets. He had no coat on, his shirt was partially tucked into tattered jeans, and his massive belly peeked through the gap. Steve was the prototypical neighborhood slob. He slipped in and out of his house each day with a scowl on his face. His house was partially painted blue over faded white aluminum siding, and trees and bushes shrouded the front of his home, obscuring the neglect. Steve also had a speech impediment.

"Looks like a mess!" he shouted before I even got out of the car.

"What happened?"

Steve launched into a slurred but astute explanation. "Because of the sufer cold weather, the froft line got down around the water main and busted it clear open. When the ground freefes it makes the pipes expand, and bam!"

I had spoken to Steve only a couple times before, and I realized I didn't know anything about the man except that he knew about frost lines, he was hard to understand, and no one ever seemed to talk to him.

"How do you know these kinds of things?" I asked him.

"I work wif metal. Done so for ofer thirty years," he answered, shirt flapping violently in the icy wind. "I saw you mof in. You like it here so far?"

"I loved it until now," I said, laughing. I was struck by Steve's friendliness. As I had watched him pull into and out of his driveway with a scowl over the last few weeks, I had assumed he was an old grouch who would be hard to relate to. Today, however, I discovered just the opposite. I said goodbye and walked past the workers into my home.

During the next few weeks I occasionally chatted with Steve while shoveling snow, getting the paper or picking up trash. One day while I was getting into my car, Steve bounded out of his front door and waved at me. I didn't know if he was just being friendly or calling me over—his mannerisms were still a bit of a mystery to me. I decided to walk over just in case.

"What's going on, Steve?"

He look down with his hands shoved in his pockets as usual. He reminded me of Eeyore from Winnie the Pooh. "I saw your gurfriend," he said. "Are you gonna get married?"

That was a strange question, I thought, but Steve was right. I had been dating my girlfriend for several months and was planning to propose soon. "Yeah, Steve, I think she's the one."

"I hope it works out fur you." He shoved his hands deeper into his pockets. "You know, I was married. My wife left me a long time ago. I've been alone efer since. We have kids but they're fur away wif their own families. I just go to work and come home now."

I stood in surprise. I had no idea Steve felt comfortable enough with me to tell me these kinds of things. I answered, "I'm sorry to hear that, Steve. You know, my door is always open and you're welcome to come have dinner with me anytime or just sit around and talk if you would like."

Steve tucked his raggedy shirt in before answering, "Thank you. That would be nice." Without saying goodbye, he turned around and walked inside, leaving me standing in his driveway, still surprised.

Steve and I continued to talk from time to time about his life and his loneliness. He even ventured over to my house a few months later, but he wouldn't come inside. He stood on the porch talking with his hands in his pockets as I sat on my porch bench and listened.

"You know, youf been awfully nice to me," he said. "I'fe liked talking to you."

This was a perfect opportunity to share the gospel with Steve. As he continued to talk, I thought more and more about sharing Christ. But right when I decided to speak up, I thought, *What if I turn him off? What if he thinks I've been nice to him just so I could talk about religion?* In the end I chickened out. I couldn't bring myself to talk about Christ, even though Steve was open and authentic with me.

After that point, the same fear gripped me whenever I saw Steve. I became so uncomfortable around him that I sometimes glanced out my window to make sure he wasn't outside before leaving the house. I could talk with Steve about the weather or water main breaks or even his loneliness and divorce, but for some reason I could not share Christ.

Over time, the feelings of fear dissipated as I gave up the idea of sharing the gospel with Steve. I stopped avoiding him, but I never spoke up about Christ either. I just stood in his driveway and listened. I would always invite him to come by, and he would always decline. Steve and I settled into a predictable, risk-free pattern of interaction.

FROZEN IN FEAR

After coming home from work one day, I sat in my living room feeling guilty about my lack of action in my neighbor's life. I prayed, "God, why do I feel the way I do?" I thought back to my first encounter with Steve, when he educated me about frost lines. I couldn't get the image of the broken water main out my mind. I sensed God showing me how I had allowed fear to control me little by little, like the creeping grip of the frost line sinking deeper into my heart. At some point, that fear began to control me so strongly that I hid behind curtains, rushed in

RECOMMENDED READING

Speaking of Jesus: How to Tell Your Friends the Best News They Will Ever Hear by J. Mack Stiles

from my car and ultimately lost my spiritual sensitivity toward Steve. The water main burst, and my heart and spirit fell under the icy control of fear.

Even though I was routinely sharing Christ with large crowds of people in churches and on college campuses, I had fallen into bondage to fear when it came to my neighbor. I learned an indispensable lesson through this experience: The most difficult people to share our faith with are those in our private spheres. When we go to school or the grocery store or a crowded sporting event, those places are part of our anonymous public life. When we return to our dorm room, our home in the suburbs or our workplace in the city, these are private worlds and we keep close tabs on what we do and say. Sharing Christ in these places is much more costly, risky, intentional and long-term.

I wish I could tell you that this story had a happy ending, but it didn't. Fear won the day. My contact with Steve decreased, his openness waned, and eventually we had little meaningful contact. As bad as the fear had been, the guilt was even worse. The devil used both of these horrible emotions to sabotage my relationship with Steve, and they are two of the most powerful weapons in his arsenal. He uses them to get us to a place where we never want to share Christ again. We're afraid of offending people, of saying the wrong thing, of losing friendships and creating awkwardness. When we allow fear to be our master, its companion guilt comes alongside and sours our taste for life on the edge.

The Christian life is fraught with fear. Jesus doesn't protect us from that fear but promises to give us the power to confront it and follow him in obedience. Each day we have a choice: give in to fear or live the adventure with confidence in his promises. I was not living on the edge with Steve. Fear and guilt led me to seek comfort and safety, but God's Holy Spirit wanted me to make an impact through faith and obedience.

UNCOMMON SENSE

Unless we deal with fear as it arises, it will sink deeper and deeper into our hearts until it controls us, making us ineffective witnesses in the lives of others.

Isn't it a shame that many of God's would-be adventurers, myself included in this instance, have bought the lie that God wants our lives to be comfortable and safe? Comfort and safety are words that relate to heaven, not the battleground of earth. It's nearly impossible to experience constant comfort and safety if we are serious about sharing our faith. But if we learn to trust Christ when we proclaim his gospel, the sit-down, strap-in, fly-by-the-seat-of-our-pants experience of being his co-adventurers will make us wonder how we could ever have considered the counterfeit alternative of living in fear.

GET THE ICE PICK OUT!

I'm sure you've been reminded in the movie theater many times, as I have, that "silence is golden." Ringing cell phones, chattering couples and packs of noisy teenagers provoke our indignation. "Didn't those people read the sign? Didn't they see the clear instructions on the screen before the movie started?"

But is silence always golden in a theater? What about the cheers when the bad guy finally gets what's coming to him? What about the gasps and mutters when the audience realizes that the murderer is really the kindly father figure? What about the laughter, the oohs and ahhs, the shrieks of surprise? In fact, without these outbursts we might conclude that the film was a failure. Silence is sometimes golden, but sometimes it's not.

When it comes to talking about Jesus at work, is silence golden? Many Christians struggle with this question on a daily basis. I have found that in the secular workplace, the long-term view is best. We must choose carefully when to talk about Jesus and when to bide our time. Unfortunately, many of us use this reality as an excuse to never speak of Christ or to speak in such generalities that our coworkers will never fully understand or respond. This was the case in my relationship with Jerry.

Jerry and I had been working together for six months. We shared a dimly lit computer room and had developed a great relationship, frequently going out to eat and spending way too much time joking around during work hours. Our favorite subject was old 1980s rap songs. "Check this out," he would say and beat out a rhyme from Kurtis Blow, EPMD, Big Daddy Kane or one of the other great fathers of rap.

"Oh yeah, well you don't know nothin' about this one," I would say, returning fire with a classic from Run-DMC, Slick Rick or KRS-1.

We carried on an ongoing competition to see who could remember the most lyrics and the most obscure songs. The funny thing was that Jerry was a small, skinny Jewish guy, and to hear him belt out the songs I grew up with as a black inner-city kid was just too much! His fearlessness about rap earned my respect and enhanced our friendship. Our relationship, however, was becoming a source of fear for me.

During the six months in which I was getting to know Jerry, I kept telling myself that silence was golden. Jerry knew I was a Christian and I knew he was Jewish, but we never talked about spiritual things. My game plan was to focus on establishing a relationship and wait patiently for the right opportunity to share Christ. The problem was that in spite of all the time we spent together and the rapport we shared, the right opportunity never came. What was more, I began to realize that introducing the subject of Christ would threaten our lighthearted camaraderie and fun times. I needed to break the ice, but I didn't know how to do it without jeopardizing the relationship. So I did nothing.

About a month later, I read 1 Corinthians 3:12-13: "Now if any man builds upon the foundation with gold, silver, precious stones, wood, hay, straw, each man's work will become evident." I sat and wondered what I was building in Jerry's life. As I thought back over the last several months, I could think of a lot of fun we'd shared, the numerous lunches, the laughs and songs, but I couldn't think of one thing I'd done to bring Jerry closer to a relationship with Jesus. As I sat staring at the page, an image of a statue came into my mind. I pictured the statue, and I began to see myself bowing down to it. I opened my eyes. "Never," I said, and got up and drove to the office.

But in the car I couldn't stop thinking about the picture. It disturbed me. "God," I prayed, "I don't have any idols in my life, do I?" As soon as I asked the question, one of my favorite oldie rap songs came on the radio and I began to get excited about surprising Jerry with this long-lost jewel. Then it hit me. My friendship with Jerry was an idol and God was using the rap song to make it clear to me. That image in my mind was of me bowing down to a relationship.

My friendship with Jerry had taken the place of my obedience to Jesus in making him known. I valued the safety and joy of our time together more than doing what was right. I didn't want to risk the relationship by making Jesus an issue, even if it meant Jerry's eternal destiny. I turned the radio off and prayed, "God, I don't know how to start telling Jerry now, after all these months. Too much time has gone by. It will be awkward. It will be hard." After I'd finished telling God all of the reasons I couldn't share the gospel, I gave up and submitted. "I need you to open a door for me, Lord," I said. I was still afraid, but by the time I arrived at the office I was determined to tell Jerry about Jesus.

I was unusually quiet coming in, taking my seat at my computer and starting to work. Jerry came in just minutes later with a big smile and said, "You'll never guess which song I heard on the way here today!"

Sure enough, Jerry began singing the rap classic I'd heard earlier, which made me laugh. He beat me to the punch with the same song the Lord had used to speak to me. I turned around and asked, "So what are you doing for lunch today?"

"Nothing. Do you want to go out?"

"Sure," I said. "There's something I'd like to talk to you about."

Jerry looked a little surprised but answered, "All right then." He took his seat and began working quietly.

I knew it, I thought to myself. *The awkwardness is already starting!* I prayed, "God, if I'm going to do this, you're going to have to help me."

The lunch hour came and Jerry asked, "So, we still on for lunch?"

"Yeah," I said, and we went down to the restaurant in our office building.

While waiting for our food, Jerry and I sat in awkward silence. He knew I wanted to talk about something serious and I knew he knew I wanted to bring something up. I finally started, "Jerry, I've really enjoyed getting to know you over these past several months and have to be honest about something. There's something I should have shared with you a long time ago."

I began sharing my personal story of faith and how God had changed my life over the years. "How does that sound so far?" I asked.

Jerry looked out the window and said, "I don't know. I don't think I've ever heard a story like that before. I'm Jewish but I wasn't raised religious—it was always just a cultural thing. We would go to synagogue occasionally, but we never talked about God or a personal relationship with him so it's just different to me."

I asked if I could share a bit more about how God had changed my life and he agreed. I wrote and drew out the gospel message on a napkin as he slurped chicken noodle soup and nervously chewed his ham and cheese on rye.

After I was finished, he said, "I think I understand what you're saying, but the one thing I've always been told is that Jesus was not the Messiah. I don't mean to offend you and you're certainly entitled to your own beliefs, but I'm just not sure who Jesus was. I've heard so many different things, you know?"

I responded, "I certainly understand that and I know this is a lot to talk about in one sitting. Can I ask you, though, if you would be turned off from talking about this from time to time? I'm not saying that I want to stop rapping and debate religions all the time, but I think this stuff is important. What if we got together once a week for lunch and continued our conversation?" Jerry seemed to like that. He relaxed and the awkwardness finally dissipated.

Jerry and I had a soup and sandwich discussion every week for nearly half a year. Our meetings were regular, planned appointments to discuss Jesus. Though regularly planned meeting are admittedly a very methodical approach, it isn't the only way. In some circumstances it's more appropriate to be flexible and ask God to give us the right opportunity to share Jesus. Whatever path we take, however, we should be moving intentionally toward more open and consistent discussions of the gospel as we develop friendships with our coworkers. We can't let fear get the better of us.

Too often we assume that people in our lives will be offended if we mention our faith. To be sure, we do sometimes lose relationships, or they are never quite the same as they were "pre-Christ." Most of the time, however, introducing someone we really care about to Christ can transform the friendship for the better. It may initially feel awkward and there may be challenges as the relationship is redefined, but we have the potential to gain a brother or sister in Christ.

How I wish that would have been the case with Jerry. The more I got to know him, the more my love and concern for him grew, and our happenstance friendship became a good friendship. We continued to talk now and then after our weekly meetings ended, and we stayed in touch even after I left the firm to pursue ministry full time. But Jerry never did receive Christ.

In some ways my relationship with Jerry was not "successful" because he didn't become a Christian. But in other ways it was successful. I conquered fear. I obeyed the Spirit's prompting. I turned the relational momentum around. I broke the ice of routine avoidance of Christ. For these successes I'm thankful. Plus, we can rarely know what happens in a human heart or what impact we've made on a person. I like to think that perhaps my relationship with Jerry broke down some negative stereotypes of Christians. Maybe some of our discussions of prophecy in the Old Testament brought him closer to recognizing Jesus as the Messiah. I hope and trust that I wasn't the last person the Lord had planned for Jerry's life. At the end of the day, I just don't know. What I do know is that I gave it my all and shared Jesus while I had the chance.

APPLICATION

As you think about your relationships at work or in other private spheres, ask yourself what the relational momentum is. Is the spiritual aspect of the relationship stagnant, growing incrementally, moving right along or red hot? Are people in your life growing in their understanding of Jesus and God's kingdom as a result of your influence? What has the effect of knowing you been on their spiritual awareness? Be honest in assessing each friendship and ask yourself these questions:

- What have I done to help this lost person move forward in understanding the gospel?
- How can I pray for this person?
- What tangible step of faith can I take to share Christ with this person?
- Who can help me think and pray about evangelism?

Put names and faces to these questions. "What have I done to help move Ravi forward in his understanding of the gospel?" "How can I more effectively and consistently pray for Jeff this week?" "What tangible thing could I do to help make sense of Jesus in Mike's mind?"

When we move from generalities to real people, we're more likely to act than if we think about the lost on an abstract level. If we regularly take stock of our relationships, we will avoid stagnation. Thinking about our friends and spending time praying for each of them greatly increases our awareness of their need for Christ.

Using the relational momentum chart, list by name the people with whom you should be sharing Christ. Include friends, neighbors, relatives, coworkers and acquaintances from your private spheres. Ask the above questions for each person on the list and begin to develop a plan to share Christ with them. It amazes me how often we make plans to go on vacation in six months but rarely plan to make sure the people around us understand the gospel.

Spend some time each week reviewing and updating your relational momentum chart. You might want to photocopy it or tear it out and put it somewhere visible—the refrigerator or the dashboard of your car. If you acted intentionally on just a few people each week, imagine the impact you could make over the course of an entire month, year or the rest of your life!

RELATIONAL MOMENTUM CHART

"For God so loved the world that he gave his only begotten Son . . ."					
Name	Relational Status	Immediate Action Step	Spiritual Preparation	Outcome	Next Step

6

SHARING IN COMMUNITY

Mr. York Moore, will you come and speak to our group?" the voice on the telephone said before any of the normal pleasantries had been exchanged.

"Who am I speaking to?" I answered.

"I'm Kevin and I'm calling on behalf of the Korean Christian Fellowship at Michigan State University."

I'd never heard of this ministry. "Let me ask you a few questions," I said. "Tell me about your group and what you have in mind."

The group was brand new and small, just twenty or so members who attended a Bible study each week. They wanted an evangelistic speaker to come in and share the gospel. I agreed and we set a date for three weeks later.

Still not knowing totally what to expect, I headed up the freeway for the hourlong drive to Michigan State. I spent the time praying and singing, beginning with the now-famous prayer, "Oh that you would bless me indeed and enlarge my border, and that Your hand might be with me, and that you would keep me from harm that it may not pain me!"

I had been praying that prayer from 1 Chronicles 4:10 for more than ten years, long before it was made popular by the book *The Prayer of Jabez* by Bruce Wilkinson. Dr. Wilkinson actually preached about this passage many years before his book became one of the fastest selling of all time.

I had been challenged in the early nineties by a sermon Dr. Wilkinson gave on the passage when he visited our church, and I committed to praying the prayer regularly. The gist of the challenge Dr. Wilkinson made in that message and in his book is that God desires to bless us so we can be a blessing to the nations. Unlike many of the self-indulgent health-wealth prayers of our day, the prayer of Jabez seeks

RECOMMENDED READING

The Prayer of Jabez by

Bruce Wilkinson

God's favor and an extension of our influence so that we can reach out with the knowledge of God's immense love. Dr. Wilkinson's ministry through that message is one of the main reasons I proclaim Jesus today. I've been challenged through this prayer to seek ever-widening influence and the adventure of a day-by-day faith as I tag along with Jesus in his work to reach the nations.

My adventure with the Korean Christian Fellowship began when I arrived at the university that evening. The group was meeting in a small, somewhat shabby house just off campus that had been converted into a ministry center by a nearby church. I arrived at the same time as the students, who spilled out of their cars laughing and taunting one another in Korean. One of the young men began to make snowballs and whip them at the others before the leader told them to calm down and come inside. We trooped into the house and I was introduced to about fifteen Korean students all at once. They were a welcoming, joyful, vivacious group of students.

"Thank you for coming," one of the women said. "We had hoped there would be more here tonight for your special message, but we are so excited that you have come. We have been praying for our friend,

Mei." She motioned to a girl sitting on the couch with some other young women. "She doesn't know Jesus yet. We have all told her she needs to become Christian but she has not. We are hoping she will become Christian tonight."

Mei was a petite girl with short black hair dyed pink at the tips and scrunched into several ponytails. She was roughhousing with her friends, and I couldn't tell any difference between her and the other students. According to the group's leader, all the others present were Christians, so I was to preach the gospel that evening for the benefit of one person—Mei. I was impressed with the passion and love the group was displaying for their friend. Her salvation was obviously their chief concern.

Before beginning, I asked for a podium or music stand to hold my notes. We looked around the house but found nothing except three mismatched cardboard boxes, which we stacked on top of one another. I remembered the prayer of Jabez. "Bless me and bless me indeed, Lord!" I prayed as I laughed at the makeshift pulpit. Looking at Mei, I prayed again: "If there is one here tonight who does not know you, Lord, let me preach as if the whole world were sinking down into the flames of hell before my eyes." Mei was worth my all that night.

It's important to recognize that God does care about numbers. Jesus saw the crowds and had compassion. God desires that his banquet hall be filled. He will not rest until every tribe, tongue and nation declares his praise. Because it's obvious that God cares about numbers, we should too. I concentrate on reaching as many people with the gospel as possible. However, Jesus didn't just minister in the major cities and thoroughfares of Israel; he made time for individuals—including those who were insignificant by society's standards. The woman at the well in John 4, Zacchaeus in Luke 19 and the Roman centurion in Matthew 8 all received Jesus' time and attention. Like Christ, we need to recognize that individuals are worth our utmost time and effort as we search for their salvation.

Not only was Mei worth my time, she was also worth my passionate energy as I shared that evening. Sometimes it's tempting to tone it down when we talk to an individual, but I think we need to exert as much energy with the one lost sheep as we would with a large crowd. The mission of every Christian given the privilege of sharing the gospel (and that's every Christian) is to do so with all our strength. We are God's voice warning the sinner not to go to that place of eternal torment and pleading with her to turn to Christ. We proclaim him as if the words from our lips were the rope pulling the sinner up from the abyss. There is no room for nonchalance.

UNCOMMON SENSE

No one is insignificant in God's eyes. Every individual is worth our pursuit.

Sometimes we're preoccupied with our performance. *What if they don't like me? What if they reject me? What if they can't relate to me? What if I mess up? What if, what if, what if . . . ?* We must get over the what-ifs and throw the rope into the abyss. Here's another analogy: If we were to pass a burning building, the difference between cowardice and heroism would be action—whether we could lay aside our fears and help rescue the people inside. Evangelism requires that we rush in with the gospel, even for the sake of one. That evening, Mei was important enough to this small community of Christians to construct an entire meeting around her, and I was honored to share in it. I had to give it my all for Mei's sake.

By the end of my message, I was sweating both from exertion and the hot, stagnant air in the old house. I asked the students to pray with me as I called for them to make a decision for Christ. "Tarrying" is what old-timers used to call this period of waiting, and we tarried for Mei. A pause after an invitation to accept Christ is just as important in individual conversations as it is with groups. Seconds can seem like minutes and minutes can seem like hours as we wait for the gospel to do its work.

Occasionally when we tarry we should encourage a decision, but other times we need to pray silently and wait. After all, once we extend the invitation, eternity stretches out before that person. She is being asked to give her entire life to Christ and forsake everything else. If that isn't clear in our explanation of the gospel, we need to go back and make it so. Sometimes following Christ means leaving a lifelong pursuit of religious good works, a family heritage, a career, an imprisoning sin or even physical safety. We must respect the sanctity of the moment of decision, step back and allow the person to do business with God. Waiting is not manipulation but respect for the individual and the work of the Holy Spirit.

THE DANCING ALTAR CALL

I didn't have to tarry long for Mei. After just a few seconds her hand shot up, eliciting gasps from several of the young people who were peeking through their fingers. I led Mei in a prayer to become a Christian, and what happened next will stay in my mind forever. As soon as I ended my prayer, at least eight of the students leapt to their feet and began to dance. They threw their arms around Mei in laughter and celebration, chattering excitedly and encouraging her for nearly twenty minutes before I had a chance to offer my congratulations on her salvation. "Mei, I will be praying for you and want you to know that I am very thankful that I was a part of your decision tonight."

"For many months, I thought about becoming a Christian," she responded. "All my friends already were, and I knew there was something different about them. They loved me, they cared for me and they prayed for me. Many of the words you spoke tonight were as if God was speaking directly to me. For a long time I have felt that I was drifting and going nowhere. I am happy tonight because I have grabbed onto the lifeline of Jesus! Thank you, Mr. York."

As I made my way toward the door, students approached me one by one, ecstatic about Mei's salvation. "We prayed so long for her and we are so glad she has become a Christian tonight," they said. "We didn't know what to do next and we are thankful you agreed to come."

I had the hour's drive back to Detroit to reflect on this experience. I realized that the vast majority of the work to bring Mei to Christ had been done before my arrival. She had become a member of Christ's community of joy and was exposed to the aroma of abundant life through her friends. That community loved her, helped her understand, prayed with her and for her. For Mei, belonging to a Christian community preceded believing what that community believed.

UNCOMMON SENSE

Many people belong to a Christian community before they believe.

We need to make room for people to join our Christian community as they walk toward an understanding of the gospel. A relationship with God can unfold beautifully over time in a communal context where members share their lives with those they are trying to reach.

During the time Mei was with the Korean Christian Fellowship, she had fallen in love with the Jesus inside the people who loved her. She witnessed the gospel through her friends, and even though that didn't give her the tools she needed to make a decision for Christ, seeing him alive in this community brought her to the precipice. All I did was come alongside Jesus in his work through the Korean community to lead Mei to Christ. When Jesus calls us to the adventure of faith, sometimes it's simply to witness the end of a work he's been doing for some time.

The American church generally makes two errors when it comes to the role of the community of faith in evangelism. The first is its belief that an unbeliever can come to saving faith vicariously through encountering a vibrant, Spirit-filled community. The Bible makes it clear that faith comes through hearing the gospel message, and herein lies the power of Christ's body. We are charged first and foremost to be God's mouthpiece in proclaiming Christ. Christ makes his appeal through us and that primarily through the proclamation of the gospel. In this sense, my ministry to Mei that evening was the indispensable capstone in a process the Lord had invited her into a long time before. I had reaped where I had not sown, but the reaping was essential for Mei's salvation.

RECOMMENDED READING

Evangelism Outside the Box

by Rick Richardson

The second error of the church is to oversimplify evangelism by merely mouthing the message of the gospel without demonstrating its reality through the love and care of the body of Christ. The words *God, faith, Jesus, heaven* and *joy* have no existential referent for people outside the community of faith. That is to say, we don't learn about who God is merely by coming to understand the word *God*. We can't just cite the Greek word for *love* and explain how it's used in a sentence. The world of relationship with God makes no sense without the community that embodies the substance of the message we proclaim.

The most effective way to do evangelism is in the context of community. The Lone Ranger approach is not the biblical norm. God wants the local church, cell groups, Bible studies, student groups and all other gatherings of Christians to be his witnessing community. The InterVarsity Christian Fellowship purpose statement states reads, "The purpose of InterVarsity Christian Fellowship/USA is to establish and advance at colleges and universities *witnessing communities* of students and faculty who follow Jesus as Savior and Lord: growing in love for God, God's Word, God's people of every ethnicity and culture and God's purposes in the world" (emphasis added). We believe God's answer for the lost on college campuses is thousands of Christian groups committed to proclaiming the gospel in the context of community—a community just like this Korean Christian Fellowship.

In the end, there is no salvation without proclamation of the gospel. At best, all our "lifestyle evangelism" produces is spiritually interested yet frustrated women and men. Only the gospel grants the power to follow Christ. Likewise, there can be no real understanding of the gospel message without it being deeply rooted in the community of joy. All too often we divorce evangelism from involvement with Christian fellowship. What is Christian evangelism that doesn't seek to incorporate people into Christ's body and pronounce to them that we can be one with Christ himself? We must, therefore, proclaim Christ and invite women and men

RECOMMENDED READING

Life Together by Dietrich Bonhoeffer

not only to relationship with Jesus but also to full identification with his body. God has chosen Christ's body to be the instrument of revolution and redemption in the earth. Without it, there is ultimately no transformation and certainly there are no dancing altar calls!

APPLICATION

The church today suffers from what I call part-time Christianity. Family, work, television, education and the pursuit of material goods preoccupy most believers, for a variety of reasons: we believe we need two incomes in the home to maintain a "normal" American lifestyle, we misunderstand the centrality of the kingdom in the Christian life, we lack real leadership in the pulpit, and we idolize the family in the evangelical church—our identity as parents supplanting our identity as Christians.

We have become an occasional group that meets for encouragement, edification, child rearing and self-enrichment. The church is supposed to be an awe-inspiring, joy-filled, living organism.

A sense of awe and joy was the most common response from people who came in contact with the witnessing community in the book of Acts. When people come into our churches today, do they experience awe and joy? Are members of your church overwhelmed with feelings of astonishment, consternation, dread or wonder? My guess is that they are not.

A large part of the problem is that we are not committed to the local church. We come in to be blessed and make friends, using the local church as a Sunday social club with day care. We do not have a sell-out mentality for reaching our community for Christ. What is your present commitment to the body of Christ? Do you serve, give, support, pray for and speak well of it? How are you supporting your pastor and pastoral staff? Do you give regularly and joyfully? How often do you pray for the mission of your church? In what ways are you serving practically? The mission of evangelism cannot be separated from the mission of the church to saturate the world with the gospel's message.

RECOMMENDED READING

Building a Contagious Church

by Mark Mittelberg

If you are not a member of a vibrant community of joy and awe, this should be your first pursuit right now. I'm not just talking about attending church but about becoming a member of the life of the community. For Mei, it was that little Korean Christian Fellowship at Michigan State University. God wants to use his body to illustrate the love of God, the joy of heaven and the sacrifice of Christ to a lost and dying world. The church cannot be that embodiment without you. God has granted you unique abilities and needs that can be carried out and met only in the context of the local church. As you find yourself becoming a part of such a community, you will begin to sense a greater measure of satisfaction and excitement in your walk with Jesus.

Sometimes the local church is far from being a community of joy. Perhaps your church is oppressed by the evil one. Perhaps politics, backbiting or a besetting congregational sin has robbed the joy from your local body. Perhaps your church is full of part-time Christians. Whatever the situation (short of theological heresy), try praying and getting involved in your fellowship before contemplating a move. God desires to send revival to the local church but he cannot do so with all the church hopping we Christians do. Give your all to the local church, for in so doing you not only live out your purpose as a Christian, but you fulfill the call to embody the gospel through the living entity of Christ's body.

PART TWO

Reaching Our World

7

REACHING PEOPLE CLOSE TO US

Damned. After realizing what it meant to be saved, I began to get a picture of what it meant to be damned. In fact, I don't think anyone can imagine what it means to be damned in the eyes of God until salvation occurs.

Think of the wisdom that comes from our mothers. Mothers want their children to look good. From the moment a baby comes home from the hospital, the mother primps and pampers it for friends and relatives; she poses and props it up for the cameras; she positions her child for success in school, family life and work. Mothers care about how their children look. But no matter how good a mother is, a day will come when her children deviate from her wisdom and protection.

I remember this coming of age in my own life around my fifth birthday when I received a pair of cowboy boots. When I laid claim to my dream boots, I vowed never to part with them—and I didn't. I wore my boots to the grocery store, to the playground, to the beach; I wore them to breakfast, lunch and dinner; I wore them to bed; I even wore them in the bathtub! How I loved my boots.

As you can imagine, after a short time my leather companions began to emit a, shall we say, curious odor. Despite my mother's pleading, plots and ploys, I would not part with my beloved boots. One of the only surviving photos from my youth shows me beside my dad's mid-1970s van in scorching summer heat wearing shorts and my cowboy boots up to my knees. God bless our mothers. As I look at that photo, I see now what my mother saw back then—I looked ridiculous! But no matter how bad I looked or smelled, I was concerned only with staying in my boots.

How much like this is our commitment to sin? The fallen nature that saturates our souls bleeds forth from every thought, action, motive and accomplishment of life. The problem is that we are blind to spiritual reality. Without Jesus, we are incapable of understanding the pervasiveness of our sin. When I was five, I didn't notice how out of place I was in my boots. I couldn't have cared less about the cloud of odor that followed me wherever I went. I didn't think it abnormal to wear leather boots in a bubble bath amidst my rubber ducky and battleships. Just like this, in our world where everyone is marked by brokenness, few people think about whether things could be other than they are.

RECOMMENDED READING

Not the Way It's Supposed to Be by Cornelius Plantinga Jr.

When I became a Christian, I was as biblically illiterate as they come. Adam may as well have been Steve, Mary Melissa, and the devil the Pillsbury Doughboy for all I knew. In those first few months the Bible was a well of comfort, an avalanche of contradictions to my thinking and a blizzard of new information. I devoured Scripture day in and day out. I would rush home from campus and sit for hours reading and rereading the stories of the Bible. I was so absorbed that my mother began to think I was ill or had fallen into a cult.

One day while I was reading the Bible, images of my mother perishing filled my head. I immediately whispered to Jesus, "Please, Lord, save my mother!" Receiving no response, I whispered a little louder, "Lord, she's my ma. Do something!" I sensed the Lord whisper back to me, "Yes, she is your mother; do something!"

Sharing our faith with people who have seen us at our worst is the most difficult kind of witness. Our families watch us go through phases and fads. They walk with us along the journey from immaturity to maturity. They've heard all our lies and self-deceptions and witnessed our mistakes. The first time I mustered the courage to sit down with my mother and share the gospel, I approached the subject all wrong—with superiority and condescension. In my mind she was the poor lost soul and I was the newly enlightened spiritual giant. Here I was, all of twenty-one, telling her about life, death, God and the meaning of existence.

We sat on our tattered rent-to-own couch for nearly twenty minutes before she politely uttered the words that would turn me inside out for the next seven years: "Rand York, I'm glad you're going through this phase. I went through it too. I went to Bible school; I've read the Bible. I already know God, and my relationship with him is a personal thing." She paused briefly. "Plus, I don't believe in original sin. I don't believe we're born bad."

I left the room and prayed, "Oh, Jesus, how do I deal with that? You must change her heart, you must."

Day after day, my burden for my mom grew. I'm convinced that brokenness over the lost is a small taste of what God experiences. If he were to give us any more than that, our hearts would break. When we join Jesus in the work of proclaiming the gospel, he changes us first. One of the reasons evangelism is the greatest adventure of our lives is that it metamorphoses us throughout the process. Evangelism benefits not only those to whom we witness but also our own relationship with God.

Over the years of talking with my mother, something began to change in our relationship—we became friends. She frequently visited my home in Detroit, saying it was a place of peace for her and that she always felt God's presence strongly there. Another interesting thing began to develop—my mother would call me up to ask questions about the Bible and request prayer. It was obvious that God was working in her heart. She was praying, reading the Bible and asking questions. I was certain her salvation was just days away. But my mother still struggled to identify herself as a sinner.

A pivotal moment came when she asked me to find her some cheap airline tickets "on that Internet thing." We sat in my home office looking at fares when all of a sudden she burst into tears, threw her head on my shoulder and began to exclaim, "I've made all the wrong choices! It's too late for me. How can God ever forgive me after all I've done?"

UNCOMMON SENSE

We, not those we seek to reach, are always changed first in the process of evangelism.

That moment of awakening in my mother produced in my spirit a wave of relief and joy as well as great pain and sorrow. God's Spirit whispered in my ear, "Speak now! She's responding to my work in her heart. Speak now!" I mustered my courage, and this time more thoughtfully began to comfort my grief-stricken mother.

"Mom," I started, "you might not be able to forgive yourself, and you can't redo anything you've done in your life, but God can forgive you and desires to do so. The whole reason Jesus came to earth was so that he could die and rise again to cleanse and deliver you from your sin."

I comforted and spoke to my mother for nearly fifteen minutes before she began to withdraw spiritually. The moment went as quickly as it came. I recognized, however, that no matter how normal our conversation was after that, she had taken an important step toward Christ. When the lost grieve over their sinfulness, they are nearest of all people outside Christ to the very presence of God.

During life's most difficult and humanly impossible moments, we get a glimpse of how insignificant and powerless we are. At these moments we are the least full of ourselves and most able to hear the voice of God. This was the case for my mother. The last year of her journey toward Christ began when her mother passed away. She and I drove down to Cleveland, Ohio, for the funeral. I was saddened by my grandmother's death but I mostly grieved for my mother. I spent the three-hour drive each way consoling her. Most of our conversation revolved around angels and heaven, which made six hours seem like ten minutes.

At one point my mom said, "Well, Grandma is in a better place. I hope I can be there someday too."

Talk about an invitation! I might have reasoned that this was no time to preach since she'd just lost her mother. I could have decided that we'd made such good progress that day that I didn't want to lose it by pressing too far. I might have even thought that I just needed to shut up and let God continue to work on her heart.

But there is no other day for salvation except the day we currently occupy. Yesterday is lost; tomorrow is not guaranteed to us. God works on people's hearts primarily through the ministry of Christians, but many are not being converted in America because we're waiting for God to "do his thing." We fail to realize that he has ordained for us to "do his thing" by using our mouths.

I jumped at the opportunity and responded, "Ma, you don't have to hope you'll be in that better place someday. You can know for sure on the basis of the Word of God." She sat listening as I shared the good news of the gospel for nearly two hours. As we approached her home I said, "Ma, is there any reason you wouldn't want to give your life to God here tonight?"

She sat silently and it was all I could do just to breathe as I waited for her response. I had been waiting for ten years. "I would like that very much," she said.

I couldn't believe it! I was scared and excited all at once. I told her I would lead us in a prayer and I wanted her to repeat it after me. I started, "Dear Jesus, I know that I am a sinner and have broken your law."

Totally ignoring my instructions, however, she prayed fervently, "Oh, God! You know I've made all the wrong choices and I'm so sorry!"

Her heartfelt prayer continued like this for some time, and I sat amazed. My mother cried out to God and came into his kingdom! I was deeply humbled and overjoyed as we sat in my car hugging and crying for some time before a final prayer and goodbye.

UNCOMMON SENSE

Successful evangelism requires willing people, not perfect people.

Many Christians are crippled by the hopelessness they feel in regard to their unbelieving family members. But Jesus himself did not have a believing family. His brothers taunted him. His mother didn't understand God's call on his life. Jesus was not only rejected by the masses in Jerusalem, his own family rejected him for years. In some families, being a Christian entails great hardship. In others faith is like the proverbial elephant in the room that no one wants to discuss. Regardless of where you find yourself, believe that God wants to use you with all your fears and imperfections to reach out and love your family in the best way you can. He desires to use you as a lighthouse to share the gospel message that can save your household.

SOMEHOW, SOME WAY

"Take I-275 south to I-75 south. Get off on I-280 south and merge onto the Ohio Turnpike going east. We'll be on that all the way until I-77 south. Once we get on I-77, we'll be on that bad boy for almost six hundred miles. Then we go I-26 east to I-95 south through Savannah and that will take us all the way to A-1 in Florida!"

According to my brother-in-law, this was the "most efficient" route from our house in Detroit to our condo on the ocean in Florida. It seemed simple enough to read, but we were about to embark on a twenty-hour-plus car ride including bathroom breaks, food stops, fillups and the occasional traffic jam and construction zone. Little did I know I was also about to embark on another evangelism adventure with Jesus.

The reality of travel always throws in some curves that disrupt even the most carefully thought through plan. Regardless of this I never begin a trip, especially an eleven hundred mile trip, without a map and turn-by-turn directions. When it comes to lost family in our lives, how much more important is it for us to have a plan to share Jesus? Many Christians have the "some-how, some way" plan, believing that their family members will hear about Jesus somehow and in some way that doesn't involve them. Unfortunately, hell is going to have many victims of this plan.

UNCOMMON SENSE

Without a well-thought-out plan to share Christ with the people closest to us, we rarely get around to doing so.

People don't hear the gospel as a result of our wishful thinking. We must lay out a plan to share Christ and be intentional about it.

Stefanie, my sister-in-law, was in the car with me on the way to Florida and we were scheduled to take a late driving shift. All four of us in the car were to take several hours at the wheel—one driver, one awake companion and two free to sleep. That put Stefanie and me in the mountains in the middle of the night. I had tried to sleep most of the day and early evening, but it was difficult with a box of crackers poking my side, 150 CDs propping up my legs and my brother-in-law barreling down the road at ninety miles per hour trying to keep our very efficient schedule. Plus, I'd been trying to come up with a plan for my time alone at the wheel with Stefanie.

Stefanie had a lot of things going for her. She came from a good home. She had a great job as a schoolteacher. She was pursuing her master's degree. She was intelligent, beautiful, funny and considerate. The only problem was that she didn't know Jesus. I needed a plan to share him with her and it kept me up when I felt like sleeping.

I didn't feel terribly confident taking spiritual action in my wife's family. Let's face it, stirring up issues in a large, tight-knit family can backfire and put a person on the outs. I was afraid that if Stefanie rejected my attempts at sharing Christ, it might produce awkwardness in the family. Like the real world of travel, an evangelistic plan is essential but often there are obstacles and bumps in the road as we navigate the adventure of sharing our faith.

When we left Detroit, the temperature was around twenty degrees— five below zero with the wind chill factor. We were happy to be traveling more than a thousand miles in the opposite direction from the frigid air. By the time Stefanie and I took the wheel that evening, we had driven far enough south that we could crack the windows and enjoy a balmy thirty-eight degrees. As the other passengers began to settle down for the evening amid empty French fry boxes and Pepsi bottles, I began to panic. I still didn't have a plan to talk to Stefanie about Jesus. Knowing that her husband might be awake and listening in the back seat didn't help matters any.

I decided to begin the conversation on a light note. Stefanie was a Michigan State University grad and I a graduate of the University of Michigan. I began, "So, Stefanie, Ron tells me you're getting your master's degree at Michigan State. Someone just explained to me why so many Michigan State grads put their diplomas on their windshields." Stefanie looked over at me, not expecting a joke. She didn't know me that well yet. I had her just where I wanted her. "It's so they can take advantage of all the handicapped parking."

Stefanie didn't seem amused at all sitting there in her dark green MSU sweatshirt. Great. I was off to a wonderful start. After several minutes of awkward silence, Stefanie graciously restarted the stalled dialogue. "I hear you're a reverend. How long have you been religious?"

From my brief interactions with Stefanie before now, I knew her to be a blunt but gracious conversationalist and had expected a curve now and then, but this threw me. "I've been called a lot of weird things in my life, but if you start calling me a reverend, we're going to have to talk about something else," I said. Finally a small chuckle. I continued, "I'm not religious in the least. In fact, I hate religion with a passion. I think religion is humankind's attempt to put God in a bottle, to control him, to use him. It's people's attempt to defang and tame an otherwise explosive power. I prefer the word *relationship*. I've had a relationship with God since December 25, 1989."

Stefanie asked how my relationship with God began and so for the next ten minutes or so, I gave her the abbreviated version of how I became a Christian. After finishing my testimony I asked, "How would you characterize your relationship with God, Stefanie?"

She looked out the window at the passing cars and barren trees and said, "I was planning to talk to you about God on this vacation, but I didn't think it would happen so quickly. We aren't even to Florida yet!"

UNCOMMON SENSE

Though our testimonies alone cannot bring people to Christ, they are a powerful tool to illustrate the power of God at work in our lives and allow others to picture themselves experiencing God.

"If you would rather wait, I'll understand," I answered.

"No," she said. "I need to do this." She began to open up, saying, "Ron and I have had many conversations about his family and their belief in God, but I have questions. I can see a huge difference in the way God is part of this family, how in almost everything and every day he plays a relevant part in their life. I grew up Catholic. I never knew someone could have a personal relationship with God. My family and friends never talked about God, how he was blessing them or how they were hearing him speak or answering prayers. God was only spoken about in church or in a swear word, never as part of everyday life."

Stefanie seemed to relax as I let her speak freely. She turned away from the window toward me and continued, "I don't pray every day. I don't consider God's will or pray for his guidance. I go to church every Sunday for Mass, but it just isn't the same as this family's faith. I enjoy the homilies, the music, the people, but it never has made much sense or meant anything to me personally. I really love my priest, Buddy. I think he has a relationship with God, I really do, but he's never explained how I could have that in my own life."

Stefanie's comments revealed the work God's Spirit had been doing in her life. She was ready and willing to talk about her longing for a relationship with him. My wife's family's witness had been an instrument to lead Stefanie to this moment where she was, as Jesus says, "ripe for harvest."

We pulled over to fill up the tank and get a couple bottles of pop—or Cokes, rather. We were in the South now, as the station attendant politely pointed out. The rest of the car woke up and peeled themselves out of their seats to stagger to the bathrooms before falling back into the car. Stefanie was also self-conscious about Ron listening to our conversation, so for the next several miles she kept asking questions to see whether he was still awake.

"Ron, did you remember to pack film?"

"Yes, Stefanie."

"Ron, do you have enough leg room back there?"

"Yes, Stefanie."

"Ron, are you asleep?"

"How can I be with you asking all these questions?"

She waited about ten more minutes before returning to our conversation. "Going back to what we were talking about, I don't feel like I have a relationship with God or even know how to go about beginning one. I feel like God is pursuing me, though. In fact, just a few years ago, I felt something was missing in my life and even tried to 'cross the line of faith,' as Ron's pastor says. But it never made any difference. I'm just confused. Do you have any advice?"

Wow! This was an open door if I'd ever heard one. I thought quickly about how to respond, glancing at the back seat once more. I decided to take things slow. "Have you ever heard the term 'being saved'?" I asked.

"Oh yeah," she said. "I heard it growing up from various people. The people who use that term are always a little weird and it creeps me out. I think it refers to someone who is overly into God, right?"

Warning. Warning, Will Robinson, I thought to myself. *Danger. Danger. Evangelistic conversation will explode in ten seconds!*

I answered, "Well, how about we think of a different term then. Imagine a relationship with God as similar to coming into a house. This house has windows and a door. Through the windows we see what God is like and what a relationship with him might look like. The windows are different ways we get glimpses of him, like through your husband's family or others who've already walked into the house and become part of God's family.

"From the things you've shared already, it sounds like you've been checking out the house and sneaking peeks into what a relationship with God might look like. Tonight God wants you to take a step of faith and walk through the door, which is Jesus." I continued explaining the gospel message, being careful to describe how Jesus was our door into the house.

I finished by saying, "God wants to give you this amazing gift, Stefanie. He doesn't want you to give him something in exchange or try to earn it because then it wouldn't be a gift. You just have to drop those things in your arms that prevent you from receiving God's amazing gift and reach out. It's for you. It has your name on it. God is giving it to you right here in the car tonight."

Stefanie and I both looked back at Ron and she said, "I want to, but I'm scared."

"Scared of what?" I asked.

She thought a minute and responded, "I just don't know what Ron and the family will think if I cross that line. Do you think they'll be mad?"

"Mad! At what?" I exclaimed. "They'd probably be so excited they'd throw a party for you. But I want you to forget about them for now. This decision is between you and God. He's standing at the door inviting you in."

"So what do I do?" she asked.

"We pray and acknowledge that Jesus died and rose again on your behalf. We pray to receive the gift and then you begin the adventure of a lifetime. Through prayer, reading your Bible and spending time with other Christians, God will begin to do miraculous things in your life. But you first have to walk through the door."

As she sat thinking, we rounded a corner and crested a hill just north of the capitol building in Charleston, West Virginia. It was lit up like a Christmas tree. The bright lights beamed forth grandly in contrast to the cold, dark mountain road behind us. As we took in the sight, Stefanie turned to me and said, "I want to do it."

I looked back again and could tell that Ron was listening and probably had been for some time. I didn't let on to Stefanie and quickly led her in a prayer to receive Christ.

Stefanie wrote to me several years later:

I want to thank you for helping me cross the line of faith that night. Accepting Jesus Christ as my personal Savior is by far the best thing I have ever done. I remember vividly your house analogy. As you spoke, I envisioned a cottage in the woods that was lit up and warm inside. It was cozy and inviting. I stood outside, wanting to go in but hesitant because of what it all meant. I was worried about Ron and my family and what they would think since I was raised Catholic. After I prayed that night, I told Ron but I was still nervous about telling everyone else. When my family found out, they weren't excited at all and for nearly four years they struggled with my faith. I think they see now how my life has changed since I got "saved" and became a true believer.

After that night I grew a lot through my conversations with other Christians. I started listening to Christian music and reading Christian books. Ron and I started going to Christian marriage seminars and classes at church. I joined a women's Bible study that opened my eyes to many things. My relationship with God is growing and he is in my thoughts daily. I pray every day, but it's never enough. I depend on the Lord; he is my rock and my strength. He pulls me through and humbles me with many blessings. I'm thankful for knowing him. It's the best decision I've ever made. I finally have peace. Thank you for helping me walk into God's "house." You've changed my life for eternity.

Your "saved" sister-in-law,
Stefanie

My plan wasn't perfect. My plan to share Christ with Stefanie was filled with ambiguity and self-doubt. In the end, however, God used my feeble attempts to help Stefanie into his house. God will use yours too. Your plan may not be entirely finished. It may have open ends, but remember, God loves our loved ones more than we ever could. The important thing is to start making a plan to reach your loved ones and give it all you've got.

APPLICATION

Have you given up on your unsaved loved ones? Has the urgency of the moment vanished in your heart? Reaching out to lost family is not easy and is often fraught with disappointments and setbacks. But don't give up. Don't grow hard and weary; trust in God and rely on him. He still wants to use you to speak the words that can change their lives. Listen for his voice and follow it. Develop a habit of prayer and fasting. Look for and create opportunities to speak the gospel to your loved ones and wait for teachable moments when they are responding to God. Be bold, passionate and hopeful, and when the time comes, call them to walk into God's house.

RECOMMENDED READING

***Out of the Saltshaker* by Rebecca Manley Pippert**

Being faithful in the work of evangelism is not just our duty and obligation as Christians, it is also how we are used by God in profound ways to change the lives of people around us, which changes us as well. It is trying but potentially the most rewarding adventure God calls us to.

If you have given up or become discouraged about reaching your loved ones, spend some time confessing that to the Father. Share with him your fears and concerns. Then get busy sharing Christ. Don't buy into the "somehow, some way" philosophy but develop a plan, pray and stay the course. It may take many months or even years before you see family members come to Christ. In fact, you may never see it happen—this is what scares us the most. Don't allow that fear to immobilize you. We are called by God to be faithful in our love and witness to our family members. Let them not only look into your house of faith, but share God's invitation to them to come into his house too.

8

REACHING PEOPLE
WE DON'T LIKE

John and Gary were the gay neighbors I tried to avoid. When they walked their dog or drove up to their home I would conveniently look the other way or at the most give the obligatory half-wave and nod, but I never went out of my way to connect with them. John was in his mid-forties, completely bald with a Buddha-like pot belly. He spoke flamboyantly with grandiose hand gestures, and his smoked glasses framed sunken brown eyes. Gary was a more confident man with a full head of gray hair, a clean-shaven professional look and a Hollywood smile.

The openness of their twelve-year relationship made me both angry and sad. The Christian mantra says we're supposed to love the sinner and hate the sin, but that's easier said than done with openly practicing homosexual neighbors. This is a story in which God taught me to do just that: to deeply love the sinner and to deeply hate sin—my own included. Sin is a soul disease that leaks out in all sorts of ways. It's not the leaking we need to worry about, but the fact that a ravening sickness is taking us all to our graves and the only cure is the shed blood of Jesus. Through understanding sin better, we can begin to understand human behavior and exercise greater grace toward those around us.

This was a hard lesson in the adventure for me but necessary for both my own spiritual maturity and my usefulness in reaching out to all my neighbors.

Shortly after I moved to this particular neighborhood, Tim, the neighborhood gossip, told me that John and Gary were the social butterflies on the block. "They throw quite a party," he said, "but I usually leave before the drunken gay sex begins."

I had been in my house for two months when I got an invitation to one of John and Gary's notorious parties. I declined the offer. For one thing, I was busy that day, and for another, I wanted to set a good example. I didn't want everyone in the neighborhood thinking I approved of gays or drunkenness. A few weeks later I spoke with Tim again.

UNCOMMON SENSE

Understanding sin as a disease helps us practice greater grace toward the people we're trying to reach.

"Yeah, John and Gary said that 'Preacher Boy' wouldn't come to their gay party. They said they were testing you to see if you would judge them," he said. While this made me disappointed and angry, I was also relieved to know that a definite line had been drawn between John and Gary and myself.

I married my wife, Jodi, a year later and together we made plans to reach out to our neighborhood as a couple. Jodi and I planned and prayed for a Christmas outreach for weeks. We made up flyers and personally delivered them to each neighbor on the block. As we visited the houses, we spent time conversing with the people who answered the door and were invited in to several homes. When we came to John and Gary's house, we rang the doorbell, waited a moment, and then I exclaimed, "Well, it doesn't look like they're home; just leave theirs in the door."

Jodi looked at me curiously as I walked off the porch—I had knocked persistently at the other houses. Nevertheless, she followed me down the stairs and back to our comfortable home. The response from the neighbors was overwhelming and Jodi and I looked forward to a full house in just a few weeks.

When the day of the party arrived, Jodi and I spent hours cleaning, decorating and preparing. We had three glittering tables of desserts laid out like something out of Martha Stewart. Scented candles, Christmas music, a decorated tree and snow on the ground—it was perfect. Suddenly the doorbell rang and about a dozen neighbors began caroling our home with "Jingle Bells." What more could we ask for our Christmas party? Nearly half the block came and it wasn't long before a cream puff-induced buzz filled the room. People were excited to be there, they were talkative, they were open, and just as the topic turned to spiritual things the door bell rang again.

RECOMMENDED READING

Welcoming but Not Affirming
by Stanley Grenz

We hadn't heard from John and Gary about the party, but there they were, standing in our living room with matching gay pride sweatshirts. I was secretly frustrated by their appearance. *What a disaster*, I thought. But we invited them in, took their coats and introduced them to everyone else. It wasn't long before John and Gary commandeered the conversation and took it away from its spiritual direction. I was not only angry but clueless as to what to do. As the party went on, I gave up on trying to speak about God. My wife and I snuck off to talk about the situation. We had purchased the *Jesus* film for each of our neighbors and had wrapped it up with a bag of popcorn.

Our intention was to give the gifts to our guests at a strategic point in the spiritual conversation, which never matured thanks to John and Gary and my fear. Jodi and I stood in the kitchen whispering. "How about just giving them the video on their way out and using that to start conversations with people in the neighborhood later?" I suggested.

"If you think that's best," Jodi replied.

We watched the night dwindle away along with my favorite baklava and carrot cake and then started showing our neighbors to the door, handing them their coats and the video. When John and Gary got ready to leave, I said, "Well, here are your coats and this is a little something from us—it's a video about the life of Jesus."

John took the video, leaned toward Gary and said softly, "This will give us something to relax with together."

"Great," I thought. "I've given them a reason to sin." I was overwhelmed with anger, embarrassment and shame.

The next few days, I couldn't get the party off my mind. I began to pray about how to proceed, and as I did my sense of shame grew. I realized that I had acted in cowardice. I had allowed John and Gary to take leadership in my own home. I had allowed two gay men to set the precedent for conversation and steer people away from hearing about Jesus. I had wasted everyone's time and a good deal of my own money. I prayed for God to forgive me for acting in cowardice, and he shook me to my spiritual core with his response. "You not only acted like a coward, you also failed," I sensed him saying. "You failed to communicate my love to John and Gary."

"John and Gary! They're the ones who ruined everything," I answered.

The *Jesus* film from Campus Crusade for Christ retells the story of the life and teaching of Jesus and gives viewers an opportunity to respond to Christ. For more information or to purchase the film, visit <www.jesusfilm.org>.

I'm usually perfectly comfortable not breaking out a full-blown gospel presentation on neighbors and friends when I spend time with them. In fact, I often make it a point to get to know people socially first, without an agenda or immediate plan. In this case, however, I was upset that the party's evangelistic purpose had been torpedoed by John and Gary's behavior—or that's what I told myself had happened.

As I wrestled with God in prayer, I became aware of several things. First, I learned that God was using this hard part of the adventure to teach me about my lack of love and even hatred for homosexuals. For as long as I could remember, I had always felt angry when speaking to or about gays and lesbians. I had used my belief in the sinfulness of homosexuality as an excuse not to show love to John and Gary. Second, I learned that God cares about all our neighbors, not just the ones I had time or concern for. Third, I learned that evangelism requires both courage and love.

UNCOMMON SENSE

Sharing our faith always requires courageous love.

Cowardice, the absence of action in the face of opportunity due to fear, and a lack of love are serious sins in God's eyes. We typically don't think of them as serious because they are passive states. We're not harming anyone, we reason. But God had blessed our party by bringing our neighbors out and giving them an interest in us and what we had to say. I had a clear opportunity to speak for Christ, and I blew it. That's serious. I allowed my fear—fear of looking judgmental and fear of failure in leading the conversation to the topic of Jesus—to determine my actions. I allowed my lack of love for John and Gary to control me rather than the Holy Spirit or the command of Jesus to love my neighbor as myself.

Jesus' story about the Good Samaritan in Luke 10 rang in my ears as I reflected on this experience. In this story, a Jewish lawyer who is seeking to justify his lack of love for non-Jews asks Jesus which neighbors he is obligated by God to love. Jesus tells him a story about a non-Jew who demonstrated his love to a Jewish man who had been beaten and left for dead while two Jewish clergymen stood by and did nothing. Jesus' point is that a lack of love and cowardice are morally equivalent to being party to deceit, violence, theft and murder. At the end of the account Jesus asks, "Who do you think demonstrated love in my story?" The Jewish lawyer answers, "The one who acted with mercy," to which Jesus responds, "Go and be like that man."

Jesus' stinging rebuke to the self-centered lawyer was God's rebuke to me about John and Gary. I passed by them on the other side of the street, justifying my cowardice and lack of love by their sinful lifestyle. A lack of initiative in the lives of our neighbors in God's eyes is as serious as playing an active part in their destruction. When we allow excuses about our neighbors' distance from God, their sin and their differences from us to prevent us from loving them courageously, we stand on the sidelines, watching them languish under the brutal hand of sin and the devil. We might as well watch them gasp their last breath while we stand next to an ambulance. We must act with courage and love to bring Christ's message of hope to people in our neighborhoods. We must, before it's too late.

Paul wrote to the Corinthian church that when he was with them, he was accompanied by three companions—weakness, fear and much trembling (1 Corinthians 2:1-5). The longer I share Jesus with lost people, the more I'm convinced that these three companions walk with me and many other Christians. What we do with our weaknesses in the light of our fear and trembling determines whether or not we faithfully carry out the work of evangelism. During the height of his career, a world-class opera vocalist was asked in an interview whether he still got stage fright. The renowned singer told the reporter, "Everyone gets stage fright, but the great singers of the world are those who can convert that nervous energy into performance energy."

I knew it was time to convert my weakness, fear and trembling into performance energy in my relationship with John and Gary. I had blind spots in my love for gays—actually, I secretly hated them. I feared John and Gary's charismatic leadership and conversational skills. I trembled at the thought of being associated with them. I needed the Holy Spirit to infuse me with wisdom, power and faith to reach them with the gospel. I began to pray, a good place to start with fear, but I prayed a safe and often ineffective prayer: "God, I ask that you would reach John and Gary. Bring Christians into their life who can relate to them and reach them with your love."

SCOOPING OUT OUR SLUDGE

A few months later I was out front scooping the last of the winter sludge of leaves and mud from my gutters. As I started down the ladder with my bulging trash bag, John came around the corner, cigarette in one hand while the other swished from side to side.

"Do you pray?" he exclaimed, startling me so badly that I dropped the trash bag. I watched it soar in slow motion to the thawing ground and hit with a slurp, splitting and spilling black sludge all over.

"What?" I asked him.

"Do you pray, being a minister and all?"

"As a matter of fact, I do. Why do you ask?" I made my way down the ladder and over the sludge to the porch, where I took off my gloves and sat down to hear the reason for John's unexpected inquiry.

"I can't really go into much detail," John began, "but I want to start praying because I'm going through some trials. I know that you're a minister and I wanted you to pray with me."

I forced the words out of my mouth. "Sure, I think that would be good—can you tell me more about what you're going through so I know how to pray?"

John paused a minute, then said, "Well, I may be facing disciplinary action at my job for something I did. There's a big inquiry going on and I'm afraid of what may happen." He proceeded to tell me one of the most debauched stories I had ever heard.

John was an instructor at a local community college, and during his career there he'd had a number of affairs with students, unbeknownst to Gary. The last relationship had been with one of his assistants. This young man, whom we'll call Ted, lived a reckless and loose life and was known as the campus party boy. John told me that Ted worked well the first semester, showing up for work on time, making good on deadlines and performing his duties up to snuff. During the first few weeks of Ted's employment, John used Ted's position, the possible exposure of his life-style, and Ted's need for male affirmation to manipulate him into a sexual relationship. This course of action usually worked for John, and Ted was no exception.

After some months Ted started to show up late for work, his duties began to go unfulfilled, and he frequently called in sick. John grew anxious and began to investigate. He showed up at Ted's house one morning after Ted had called in sick. Ted was at home, and John invited himself in. After a few pleasantries, John convinced Ted to go to bed with him. After this encounter, Ted finally put his cards on the table. He was HIV-positive, and not only that, he had purposely pursued the assistant position in order to blackmail John, threatening to expose to the college what he had been doing. "I'm afraid of what may happen at school and what may happen to me with Gary," John finished.

I sat dumbfounded. John's life was like the trail of sludge seeping from the bag in front of us. That sludge was also like what was leaking out of my own heart toward John. I felt dirty inside as John spilled his problems out to me. But God was starting to clean up the gunk.

"Have you ever studied the Bible?" I asked.

"Yes," John responded. "In fact, I write spiritual poetry for church sometimes."

"I wondered if you and I could get together to look at the Bible and pray. We could start what I call a GIG, which stands for a group investigating God. A GIG is a laid-back way of discussing spiritual things using the Bible as our guide."

I've found GIGs to be an excellent way to reach people over a short period of time in a relaxed and relational context. "Do you have a Bible?" I asked.

"Sure do! What day works for you?"

I couldn't believe it. I was setting up a six-week GIG commitment with my gay neighbor. We established a date and time and John went as he came, hand swaggering, smoking his cigarettes.

My GIG with John began a couple of weeks later and by then it was spring. I had the windows open and the first sweet smells of spring saturated my living room. Despite the benign weather, I was nervous. No turning back now, I thought. Right on time, John started walking down the street. He had a giddy look on his face and was sporting baggy shorts and an oversized button-down shirt. A beat-up Bible was tucked in his

GIGs (groups investigating God) are fifty-minute weekly discussions where guests commit for four to six weeks to look at Jesus and his teachings using the Bible. GIGs were created by InterVarsity Christian Fellowship as a relational way to reach college students with the gospel but have been adopted by many as an excellent tool to reach out to neighbors, coworkers, friends and relatives. For more information about GIGs or for resources, visit <www.ivcf.org> or <www.ivpress.com>.

arms and he walked much more directly than I was accustomed to seeing. He marched confidently up to the door and rang the bell. "Hey, John! Come on in," I said.

"I brought some of my poetry for you to read," he said.

"Great," I responded, "Let me take a look at it."

It's important for us to take leadership in our meetings with lost people but never so tightly that we create an artificial or forced atmosphere. Particularly when we meet for the first or second time, we should be prepared to go with the flow. John was obviously excited that I would read his poetry and encouraged me to hold on to it for a while to think about it. I was sincerely honored.

We started our first GIG by studying Luke 15, which contains the parables of the lost sheep, coin and son. In this passage Jesus is talking to two groups of people. On one side is a group of hardened sinners who have begun to trust Jesus and listen to his teachings on the kingdom of God. On the other side is a group of hardened religious folk who have become increasingly hostile and distrustful of Jesus. Jesus' stories reveal a radical departure from traditional thinking on the part of both the sinners and religious people about God and his love for his children. In the climax, Jesus paints a picture of a man who has lost two sons—one to the lure of fast living, sexual gratification and worldly possessions, and the other to duty, frustration and anger. One son physically leaves his father to live a life of open rebellion. The other son stays home but distances himself, basing his relationship with his father on obligation and performance.

Upon the return of the rebellious son, the father runs to him, falls on his neck, reinstates him and throws an extravagant party. When the dutiful son sees this, he's enraged. He won't come in to the party and won't even speak directly to his father. The father tries to reason with his son, explaining that the party is necessary because his son has virtually come back from the dead. He also tells the dutiful son how much he loves him and how everything he possesses is available to him. In this story Jesus is portraying God's love for all his children. The sinners are astonished to learn that their heavenly father could receive and celebrate those who have lived so sinfully. The religious folk are amazed to learn that God sees them outside of the party instead of at the head of the table and perhaps even outside of a relationship with him.

As we read, John stopped me and said, "Wait a minute! What you're saying is that the father—who is obviously God here—waits and longs for people to come back to him no matter what they've done and that religious people don't make the grade?"

Here is the beauty of GIGs. John had eloquently and in his own words articulated a major truth of this passage. Not only that, he was demonstrating a personal resonance with that truth.

"I'm not saying that, Jesus did," I responded. "What do you think about that?"

John continued, "I don't know. I'll have to think about that one. When I think of God, I think more like the religious leaders. I mean, it just makes sense that if you go to church and pray that God will accept you, but it seems like that's not true according to this passage." I've known seminary students who couldn't describe this text more accurately or poignantly than John had in just a few sentences.

John and I continued to meet together throughout the summer, studying the Bible and praying in the afternoons in my shaded, breezy living room as the neighborhood looked on. I cared less and less how things looked between John and me as I saw God working in some miraculous ways. John came exactly on time each week. He did the homework I assigned him. He even got upset when I had to reschedule our GIG because of travel.

The situation at John's workplace continued to fluctuate as he dealt with the fallout of the student's quest to expose him. John, however, was decreasingly concerned about those issues and it seemed they would die down soon. John also discovered that he had not contracted HIV from Ted, even though their last sexual encounter had been unprotected.

John was taking baby steps toward God and I was seeing it happen before my very eyes. One afternoon my neighbor Tim stopped me outside across my backyard fence and asked, "So what are you and John doing? I see him coming over all the time."

UNCOMMON SENSE

Intentionally contradicting people's expectations of what a Christian is, says or does catches people off guard and can produce intense interest.

Here it was—the hour of reckoning. I took a deep breath, prayed and responded, "John and I have been studying the Bible each week. It's been great!"

My excitement took Tim by surprise. "Oh, well, that's great," he said. "I'm a little surprised that John would study the Bible, being gay and all."

This remark provided an opportunity for me to share the good news of Jesus with Tim. He had heard the gospel from me before, but now there was a point of confusion. When we contradict people's expectations of what it means to be a Christian, this dissonance creates one of the best situations in which we can help them consider Jesus.

Tim's understanding of Christians was that we hated gays, protested the gay lifestyle and would have nothing to do with gays aside from telling them they were going to hell. Much of that perception would have been true of my own life had God not given me a love for John. John was still locked in sin and rebellion against God, but I had been freed to love him.

My last GIG with John before the summer ended focused on the story Jesus tells in Luke 18 of a religious leader and a tax collector who go up to the temple to pray. The religious leader prays with confidence, even arrogance, bragging to God about what he has done. The tax collector, convicted of his sin, prays almost despairingly, lamenting and asking God to be merciful to him.

"If we are going to have a relationship with God, John, we must acknowledge our inadequacy before God," I said. "We have to call on God for mercy and look to what he's done on the cross through Jesus to provide forgiveness for sin."

As I continued explaining the gospel, John looked as if the Holy Spirit had him by the ear. Typically when someone is under conviction, they appear to be in a struggle for their life. John was in the throes of this struggle and I pressed on. "We've been studying for some time now, but I think God wants you to take the next step. This study and this message are not like the others we've looked at. I believe God is speaking and calling you personally to make a decision today about your sin and your trust in Jesus."

RECOMMENDED READING

Soul-Winner: How to Lead Sinners to the Saviour by Charles Haddon Spurgeon

When I referred to John's sin, I was not alluding to his sexual transgressions. In fact, I don't believe sharing Christ with gays and lesbians needs to center on convincing them that their lifestyle is sinful. We need to help them understand their underlying sin sickness and realize that they have broken God's laws in many ways. I use the ten commandments to do this (more on this later) because I believe the moral law of God is still a tutor to lead us to Christ (Galatians 3:24). Using God's moral law helps us lead people to see the sin sickness without alienating them by feeding into anticipated stereotypes.

For the first time in our relationship, John cracked. The veneer of confidence and self-reliance broke. "After I went to college I looked for

God," he started. "I wanted a relationship with him but I was angered and turned away by the Christians I tried to get to know."

John's eyes began to well up. "I decided that I would run as far away from God and Christians as I possibly could," he continued, "but then you moved here. I've been seeing God in our friendship and in the Bible, but I just don't know."

John and I talked and prayed that day for some time. He never made a decision to become a Christian or to leave Gary, but while I lived in that neighborhood, God blessed us with a good friendship. I believe John was confronted over the course of that friendship time and time again with the person of Jesus and his call for him to repent and find life.

Eventually John and I lost touch when I moved nearly an hour away, but I have to believe that if nothing else happened, John lost his rigid, determined hatred for Christians and legitimately encountered Jesus and the beauty of the gospel. In addition, God used John in my life to make me more like Jesus. Just because the adventure of evangelism primarily moves from the Christian to the lost does not mean that positive influence doesn't flow from the lost to the Christian. In fact, that's exactly what happened when Peter shared Christ with Cornelius in Acts 10—God dealt with Peter's racism. In the same way, God used a conniving, arrogant, decadent gay man to break me of my lack of love, to reveal my weaknesses in evangelism and to bring an end to some of my fear and trembling.

APPLICATION

As you think about your own weakness, the fears and apprehensions that hinder you from sharing Jesus with your neighbors, consider not only what God can do if you allow him to work through you but also what he can do as he works in you. I learned that, yes, God wanted to reach John and Gary with the gospel, but I almost missed the blessing he had in ridding me of my hatred, fear and distrust of gays. Do you avoid getting involved with certain people in your life because of these same reactions? Are they people of a different culture, color or ethnic group? Are they richer or poorer than you? Do they hold different political or ideological views? Are they obnoxious, insulting or hard to talk to? Ask God to reveal these areas of weakness and to work in you to bring the gospel to these challenging people.

Second, have you allowed your familiarity and comfort with certain types of people to become an excuse for a lack of growth? God cares about all who are lost and we do not have the luxury of playing favorites. I've found that when I try to excuse myself from reaching out to certain categories of people, those are exactly the people God brings into my life to challenge me. One of the most frightening things we can do is ask God to move us out of our comfort zone, but that's exactly what I want you to pray right now. Ask God to bring about a set of circumstances with a person or group of people that will stretch who you are. Don't just ask God to use you to reach lost people; ask him to use lost people to reach you, to change you, to increase your compassion and understanding of the world for which Jesus died.

Third, knowing that evangelism requires both courage and love, ask God to give you boldness and reach out to those around you no matter who they are. You may want to refer to the list you made earlier and reflect on it during a time of prayer. As particular people and opportunities become available to you, take the risk of showing love. This is the real risk. It wasn't a risk, as I discovered, to have John come into my home. It wasn't a risk to have John come into my life. It was a risk to have John come into my heart. Don't miss out on the blessing of having lost people so touch your heart that you are changed as much or more than they will ever be.

9

REACHING PEOPLE WHO DON'T LIKE US

Mondays—how I loved them! I loved the smell of hot toner in the copy machines, the sight of people sweeping from office to cubicle and back like square dancers at a hoedown, the sound of my peers moaning about how they failed their diets once again. I loved the huffing of my supervisor as she paced in and out of her office with wrinkled brow, communicating to us all that important work needed to be done. Most of all I loved the post-weekend office chatter. I was working at a market research firm as a statistical analyst in a department with about fifteen other entry-level coworkers. For the most part, we all had high aspirations and a competitive spirit. Most of us were just three years or less out of college, all bucking for the same promotions and recognition, all climbing the proverbial ladder of success.

Each Monday we would try to outdo one another with what we were buying or doing with our lives. Inevitably someone would mention a house they were looking at, a new SUV parked out front, designer clothes, a future vacation, an expensive gadget, a lucrative investment. Even though I knew these were worldly measures of success and God cared more about how I used my income to bless his kingdom, I admit that I took part in the materialistic bragfest with the rest of them. I rationalized my preoccupation with affluence by telling myself how "spiritual" I was. I gave more than 10 percent to church and other ministries, I gave my time and energy, I ministered to the poor and homeless. Wasn't I entitled?

Besides, I didn't want to be different—not yet, anyway. I wanted to fit in and move up. I wanted a position of authority in the company before I made Jesus an issue. The problem was that I already had all the authority I needed to influence people for Christ—it came from being God's child. Furthermore, the sin of entitlement was preventing me from making a difference in the lives of people around me. I was stagnating in the adventure. When God's children need to get out of a spiritual rut, God often uses the most offensive people to help us along. We need only remember Israel's exile to Babylon. God used a godless empire to humble his people and bring them back to full reliance on him. I was looking to worldly influence and power to give me significance, but God wanted to use Linda, the most offensive and godless person in the firm, to give me faith.

Linda had been in our department the longest and was first in line for the next step up. She was also the office flirt and daydream of most of the firm's male employees. She wore stiletto heels, tight, flashy dresses that pushed her breasts up and forward, and heavy eye makeup with bright red lipstick. Everyone knew she didn't mean anything by her overtures, but nevertheless I tried my hardest to avoid her. This particular Monday, however, was the day Linda changed everything for me at the company. She swayed over to my cubicle, leaned over and seductively whispered, "What did you do this weekend?" She paused and then added, "Church boy!" The cat was out of the bag.

Linda had overheard me praying with another Christian in the next department before most people arrived that morning and rightly concluded that I was one of those dreaded Christians. I ignored her question and the dig and asked, "What did you do?"

"I went to the bar with my husband and got drunk," she replied, staring at me brazenly as if to say, "So what do you think about that?" Not
receiving a response from me, she swaggered off. Throughout the day,
Linda talked loudly about anything and everything that would normally
offend religious people. She could do whatever she wanted now. She had
the admiration and respect of her peers, the boss seemed to like her and
she'd been there the longest. What's worse, Linda had it out for me big-
time. I had no idea what to do.

As the Mondays went by, I became less interested in the office gossip
and less happy with my job. Linda become more blatant in her attempts
to rattle me; even the others began to notice the unspoken war between
us. Just before lunch one day and without provocation Linda finally
spoke her mind. She let loose with a long string of obscenities and said,
"I can't stand Christians. I wish they were all dead." She stormed out of
the room as everyone sat stunned, staring at me.

Adrian, one of my coworkers, asked, "What's going on? Did you do
something to her?"

"Nothing at all," I responded. But I began to think about the question.
Had I done something to her? I was sure I hadn't. As I sat in the lunch
room with my belly full of bees, it dawned on me. Linda was angry at
someone—someone with whom I most likely had a lot in common. Was
it a pastor? Did a Christian relative betray her somehow?

Even though I had been humiliated by Linda's behavior over the last
several weeks, I needed to get to the bottom of it. People's pain is often
masked by hostility. When we experience antagonism focused on our
faith in Christ, it should signal us to go the extra mile and begin to probe
for an underlying explanation. Recoiling in fear or responding with similar hostility does not advance the kingdom of God. We need to speak
for God and make an appeal for his pursuing love.

That afternoon Linda was sitting in a vacant office by herself looking
out the window. This looked like the perfect opportunity to ask her why

she had said what she had about Christians. I rushed in without thought or prayer. "Linda, what you said before lunch hurt my feelings. I wondered if we could talk about it."

My motives were sincere. I was trying to communicate honestly and clearly. But it didn't work at all.

"You can go to hell for all I care," she spat out. "All you holier than thou hypocrites can just go to hell." She brushed past me and returned to her cubicle.

Whoa! What just happened here? I asked myself.

From that moment on, it was all out-war. Each time I would speak, Linda would sigh. If I got up to go to the bathroom, she would huff. I was angry too, and I theologized my resentment to justify my feelings. *She's keeping me from teaching my coworkers about God*, I told myself. *She's bringing dishonor to the name of Jesus. The Bible says not to throw your pearls before swine, which she obviously is.*

These excuses, combined with my prayerless approach to the situation, allowed my anger and hostility to grow. The only problem was that I couldn't get Linda off my mind. I thought about her when I drove home. I thought about her when I ate dinner or went to the movies. I thought about her when I went to church. I lay awake at night thinking about her and the trouble about to unfold the next day.

One day after Sunday morning service, I asked my friend John to pray for my mental vexation, which really got me into trouble. John had a bigger heart for people than I did. He was an outside observer who had not been embroiled in the hand-to-hand office combat of the last few months. Most of all, he was being used by the Holy Spirit to speak directly to me. John prayed, "Lord, thank you for putting Linda in York's life to help bring him to greater dependence on you. I pray that you would use this situation to speak to her about her need for Jesus and to York about his need for you to deal with the circumstances."

There it was: the simple wisdom that I had encountered before but quickly forgotten. The battle I was in was no easy battle. It wasn't merely about my coworkers; it wasn't just about Linda's eternal destiny. The battle was also for a greater piece of my heart and soul. How I loved and hated Jesus simultaneously at that moment. I was angry at him for messing up my indulgent and comfortable office life. I didn't appreciate that he had made my faith an issue at the time he did. I didn't understand how he could use such a hostile pagan to mold me. I was angry for the roundabout way in which he was revealing his lesson for me.

UNCOMMON SENSE

Having friends pray with and for us as we reach out to unbelievers is an important part of our growth in the adventure of evangelism.

I was angry but convicted. I knew that every single person needed to hear about Jesus, Linda included, and I was God's representative in Linda's life right now. Regardless of the consequences, it was my responsibility to pursue Linda, not merely tolerate her. That night I laid Linda and my situation before God as I had never done before. I prayed for my attitude. I prayed for her resistance. I prayed for my coworkers. I prayed for boldness and wisdom in pursuing a relationship with Linda.

Monday. I sat at my desk with the toner burning, the people whirling and my supervisor huffing, but my mind was on one thing alone—Linda. I was resolved to speak with her, but I was terrified. I watched her all day, wondering how and when to start the conversation. As I sat not doing much work, visions of my own beheading and castration racing through my mind, Linda suddenly snuck up behind me and asked, "Do you want to come to the bar with us after work?"

Of course, she didn't really want me to come to the bar, nor did she think I would; this was her way of razzing me. I looked up to see everyone in the department staring at me, wondering how I would handle this one. I asked, "Where are you going?"

This was not the response Linda had expected. Instead of the quick shrug and habitual "no" I usually gave, I was showing some interest. I couldn't believe it either.

"About ten of us are going to this restaurant for drinks after work—you don't want to go, do you?" I could tell she was somewhat nervous about my sudden change.

"I think I'll join you," I said as my coworkers shot each other looks of disbelief.

I was starting to learn that when it comes to getting inside the real world of everyday people, we have to meet them on their own turf. I'm not suggesting that all Christians start going to nightclubs and bars on a regular basis. But each and every Christian needs to find a time and place to meet lost people in their domain. This might be their home, the gym, a concert or a sports arena. If all we ever do is invite people to church, we aren't following Jesus' example. He went from village to village, the domain of regular everyday people, to proclaim the kingdom of God. This can be scary—it was for me—but often when we step into the world of lost friends, we see real progress in the adventure of evangelism.

UNCOMMON SENSE

Spending time with people in a place where they feel comfortable is a profound way to shift the dynamics of the relationship and earn trust.

JESUS GOES TO THE BAR

We got to the restaurant around 6 p.m. and Linda ordered a tequila and beer. The others followed suit, ordering fuzzy navels, rum and Cokes,

Bud Lights. I, like a corny sitcom character, said, "Diet Pepsi, please."

Everyone laughed and Linda weighed in, "Just what I thought. Preacher boy isn't really going to drink with us."

We spent the next ten minutes or so talking about Christian liberties and alcohol, which led to talking about the pope, which led to bad pope jokes, which led to conversation about sex, which led to gossip about our supervisor, and so on and so on and so on.

I left around 7:30, thanking them for asking me to join them. Linda responded, "Yeah, yeah, preacher boy, leave before the real fun starts. We'll see you tomorrow."

Even though it was a dig, the nagging bite was gone from her voice. She seemed to be joking with me as she would with the others. Once in my car I giggled like an eight-year-old girl. "Thank you, Jesus, for going to the bar with me!"

Even though it seemed that nothing was really accomplished in the souls of my coworkers, I had made the first move into Linda's world. I had stepped out of my comfort zone and joined Linda in a place where she was in control, where she made the rules, where she was top dog. I had known Linda for nearly a year, but my relationship with her began that night in a bar over tequila and Diet Pepsi.

The next morning I came into the office hopeful but sober-minded. I knew there was a long road ahead in terms of reaching my coworkers. The day played out uneventfully. Linda got in a couple of jabs—it was her obligation to keep up her image as the resident iconoclast. Several days later, she and I were assigned to an important and complicated project that required us to work long hours alone together. During the first couple of days there was a lot of awkward silence as people passed by, glancing in to see if we were at each other's throats. Surprisingly, though, there were also pleasant moments when we talked about movies and television shows.

One day in the middle of the project, Linda asked, "So do you believe in hell and angels and devils and all that stuff?"

This was the first sincere inquiry Linda had made concerning my faith—but what to say? I didn't want to blow it or have her storm out of the room again. This time I responded with a little more wisdom, saying, "That's an interesting question," and pausing just long enough to pray, "What do I do now, Lord?" He brought an image to mind of Jesus being questioned by the clergy of his day and answering their question with a question. I decided to try that.

"Let me ask you first what you believe about 'all that stuff,'" I said.

Linda began to speak and didn't come up for air for nearly ten minutes. I sat riveted to every word. She talked about how she and her best friend in college used to live it up on the weekends, partying and meeting guys. With irritation and even hatred in her voice, Linda then recounted how an evangelist visited their campus frequently and yelled at the students as they walked to and from class. Her story revealed why she had been so angry with me these last several months. "He would yell out 'sinner!' and 'slut!'" she said, "but my friend and I just walked on."

Linda continued, "Then one day I ran into my friend and she was dressed funny. She had cut her hair and taken off all her makeup and jewelry. She told me I was going to hell because I wore skimpy skirts, listened to rock music and drank. She told me she couldn't hang out with me anymore since she had joined this preacher's church. Ever since then, I've vowed never to listen to a thing any preacher had to say."

I was right. Someone had hurt Linda very badly. She painted a picture of deep pain, anger and resentment at the loss of someone who mattered to her deeply. I said, "Linda, that's a terrible story. I want you to know that I feel badly for your loss."

Linda sat silently, visibly shaken from dredging up the old emotions of her past. We talked for nearly an hour about this so-called evangelist and his cult. Linda was surprised to hear that real Christians don't believe the things this man and her friend had taught her. I explained how their church, which is prominent on college campuses across the nation, actually teaches a perversion of the good news of the Bible.

Linda couldn't wait to hear what I believed. Unfortunately, the day was over and everyone was leaving to go home. I ended our conversation by saying, "I've really enjoyed hearing your perspective on these things; maybe we can talk again about them another time."

She agreed and we walked out of the building together, to the amazement of everyone in our department. I jumped in my car and headed down the road crying as I prayed, "Lord, thank you for using me. I pray that you would use me to overturn Linda's anger and resistance to you. Take our conversation and cause her to wrestle with it tonight."

The next day I took about twenty minutes to carefully explain the gospel message. I prefaced my remarks by saying, "Linda, I want you to know up front that I do believe that we are all sinners, and because of that we all deserve eternal separation from God in a literal place called hell. However, you should know that this is not God's desire nor is it his intent to allow us to go to hell without a fight."

I went on to explain how Jesus' life on earth, his death on the cross and the victory of his resurrection were God's way of engaging the fight against sin, death, hell and the devil. I particularly camped on the idea of sin as a disease. "In the Bible, the Greek word for sin leads us to an understanding of sin as a disease. This disease has certain symptoms, which are the ways we break God's moral law. Sin should be understood as a deep and deadly sickness rather than flaws in our character or random bad thoughts and mistakes that need to be checked once in a while."

Linda responded, "So you're saying that Jesus' death on the cross is able to heal us from this disease."

She had perfectly articulated what I was about to say. "Yes," I answered, "and what's more, if we allow God to heal us and to wipe our record clean, he gives us a kind of supernatural power to live life the way it was intended—abundantly. He wants to give us the ability to learn how to live right. He also changes our appetite for sinful behavior over the course of time if we allow him to do so."

"That sounds great to me—if it's true," Linda said. Her response was not one of rejection but of interest.

After this conversation, Linda and I continued to discuss the gospel at least a couple times each week. Our short exchanges seemed to bring Linda noticeably closer to understanding Jesus and his kingdom. She would come to work with questions, some of which required me to do research, but I didn't mind. I was seeing God at work in her heart and it was beautiful. The conversations between Linda and me often included other colleagues, and our reconciliation struck awe in the department—it was a great time of faith and influence in the company and also in my life. God had used Linda to bring me back into the adventure and to correct my focus. Mondays were no longer self-indulgent bragfests, but the start of a week of ministry to my coworkers.

Another Monday. A dark cloud hung over our mirrored glass building as I pulled up to work. The moisture in the air was as thick as gravy. It was the last warm day of fall, and a storm was brewing as I took my seat in my cubicle. I didn't smell the toner burning and everyone seemed to sit listlessly in their seats as the storm broke outside. Suddenly Linda came rushing in, drenched from the heavy burst of rain. She was sobbing uncontrollably as she went into our supervisor's office and shut the door. Everyone sat in shock for a moment but soon began to mutter about what could have happened.

About fifteen minutes later, Linda emerged, collected some things from her desk and walked out of the building. Our supervisor came to her door and told us, "Linda's husband has contracted a rare neurological disease and is in the hospital unable to move. The disease will require him to relearn everything from eating to walking, so Linda will be out for several months."

My heart sank along with everyone else's. Linda might have been a loud, obnoxious flirt, but she was loved. I had grown to appreciate her candor and her secret, sincere questions. Linda had been making real progress toward Jesus—and now this.

During the next several months Linda popped in and out of the office to pick up work to take home with her. Her husband's recovery was hard, costly and emotionally taxing, and it was taking its toll on her. One day when she stopped in to drop off a project, I had an opportunity to speak with her. "How are you, Linda?" I asked.

UNCOMMON SENSE

How we speak is as important as what we say.

"I never thought I would have to go through anything like this," she said. "You know, during this time I've thought a lot about everything we've discussed about Jesus. I want to thank you for helping me let go of my anger, and more importantly, I want to thank you for helping me with my relationship with God."

Linda had not made a decision yet to become a Christian, but she had come a long way. I nearly cried as I said goodbye to her. I was leaving the firm to go into full-time ministry, and she said these final words before leaving: "Thanks for everything you've done—I hope you do well as a preacher."

Those words meant more to me than she could have realized. I lost contact with Linda after that, and though I didn't have the joy of seeing her come to faith in Jesus, I had the joy of being her friend.

What would have happened if I had given up on Linda? What would office life had been like if I had taken a combative stance? What if I had never taken the risk of asking her what she thought about "all that stuff"? God had used the tension and hostility of an unforgiving coworker to bring me to a place of understanding. Through Linda, I came to understand that I was God's voice in the department where I worked. I realized that how I spoke was just as important as what I said.

I learned that God's timing in the adventure may not be convenient or comfortable, but it's right. I learned that people's anger often has a history, and that history must be taken seriously. I also discovered that it's worth the risk to step out of our comfort zone and come alongside someone, even at the risk of total rejection and humiliation.

APPLICATION

We should never see people as the enemy, even when they're hostile and resistant. Behind every façade of hostility is pain, and every supposed adversary is a potential friend and target for God's pursuing love. Are there Lindas in your life that you've given up on? Are there people who are hard to get along with, who rub you the wrong way, who offend you either inadvertently or on purpose? Let me exhort you not to give up.

RECOMMENDED READING

If You Want to Walk on Water, You've Got to Get Out of the Boat **by John Ortberg**

What have you done to find out why these people are the way they are? What would it look like for God to open a window of opportunity in such a way that they are forever changed? Not every person will respond like Linda. Many people, the Bible says, will continue on their way to hell and nothing we do will stop them or even slow them down. But many people will, in the face of love and persistence, crack the window of their soul just wide enough for you to peer in and assess the damage.

Let me give you two challenges. First, ask God to give you his perspective on your role in people's lives. You can even steal my friend John's prayer: "Lord, thank you for putting _____ in my life to help bring me to greater dependence on you. I pray that you would use this situation to speak to _____ about his need for Jesus and to me about my need for you to deal with this circumstance." Ask God to help you see hope and the possibility of change when you meet difficult people. Finally, ask him to give you wisdom when taking steps of friendship.

Second, I challenge you to take at least one tangible risk today. Is there a neighbor, coworker or relative in your life with whom it would be risky to talk about Jesus? Why don't you pick up the phone, walk down the street or send out an e-mail and invite them over for dinner, out for coffee, to the gym or whatever—just step out and try. There are few certainties in evangelism, but there is one money-back guarantee: if we don't even try, we have already failed.

10

REACHING PEOPLE WHO HAVE IT ALL TOGETHER

A dense haze had settled over the city like a warm, wet towel after the cold Michigan sky dumped eight inches of snow overnight. The streets had become a slushy mix of snow and water, and the precipitation was now trickling down the street and pooling around the gutters. As I stood gazing at the wintry scene, Dan pulled into my driveway in my dream car—a sleek, silver luxury sedan with light-tan leather upholstery and tinted windows. It was spotless and glistening, somehow defying the ice, mud and snow that encrusted everything else. Dan was my new financial advisor and, like his car, his life seemed spotless and glistening.

I had known Dan a couple of months and even though we got along great, I felt out of my league around him. Just to look at him and hear him talk about money made me feel like a student, even though I was older. Dan had sparkling eyes and white teeth that were so well-aligned I wondered if they were real. His wife was a svelte size six with immovable hair, manicured nails and showcase clothes. His son was a boisterous, ruddy five-year-old with amazingly crystal-blue eyes. Dan was always perfectly pressed, perfectly polite and perfectly punctual, and this morning was no exception.

As Dan sat in my living room discussing life insurance and mutual

UNCOMMON SENSE

Every person, no matter who they are, needs Jesus and needs to hear the message of God's unceasing love.

funds, my mind began to wander. Did people like Dan need Jesus too? What could possibly be missing in his life? Would a relationship with God make any difference?

Theoretically I knew Dan needed Jesus; no matter what I was seeing on the outside, he had a sin problem that only Christ's death and resurrection could address. His life would indeed be different if he knew God. It was difficult, however, to believe he needed the gospel in a tangible way and even more difficult to know how exactly to share it with him. Sometimes I feel like I have nothing to offer the people God brings into my life, and Dan was a prime example.

As I brought my attention back to Dan's polished presentation I said, "That sounds great, Dan. Thanks again for helping me with all this."

He was assisting me in an area about which I had very little confidence or knowledge. Like many Christians, I often don't stop to think about sharing Christ with people who are my superiors. Schoolteachers and professors, supervisors, parents, loan officers, politicians, doctors—these people occupy places of authority. Authority can challenge our confidence, rattle our cages and call our faith into question. I believe, however, that every single person, no matter who they are or what they do, needs to hear the gospel message. Every person matters so much to God that he will not cease until they know of his love.

Dan drove off as smoothly as he had come, and I went back to gazing at the mystical scene of dripping trees and rooftops. As I stared into space, God's Holy Spirit asked me a question. "What are you going to do to reach Dan?"

I responded out loud. "What are *you* going to do, Lord? If Dan is going to hear and respond to Jesus, he needs much more than I have to give!"

Have you ever noticed how God's answer often comes from our own lips? As quickly as it had come out of my mouth, I realized that of course I didn't have anything to offer Dan. I was convicted. "Lord, I'm sorry for thinking I could reach anyone with my own talents or gifts. I know that if Dan is going to learn about Jesus, it will have to be you working through me. Forgive me, Lord."

That morning, as a result of my encounter with God through prayer, the Holy Spirit drew me under greater control. Having a mind that is subject to the Spirit is essential to reaching people with the love of Christ. When under the control of God's Spirit, we will possess the confidence, knowledge and determination to properly share Jesus with anyone around us—whether a homeless person or flashy financial advisor.

UNCOMMON SENSE

Reaching people with the message of Jesus is always a work of the Holy Spirit and does not depend on our talents and abilities.

If we stop and think about what evangelism really is, we have to conclude that the only way it happens is through the power of God's Spirit. When we explain the gospel, we are essentially saying that all of us abide under God's holy wrath because of our sin and that our only recourse is to totally and unequivocally place our trust in his righteous Son, Jesus Christ, and his death and resurrection on our behalf. We must profess our intent to follow Jesus into a life of self-denial and sacrifice whereby we are promised true life.

It's an amazing and offensive message with no room for demands or alternatives. We are speaking a "thus saith the Lord" kind of message. We are requiring people to abandon the person they are and leave the path they're on in order to receive life. This requires the work of God's Spirit.

Of course, there are many ways to communicate this message and we must be savvy in discerning how best to approach each of these truths with particular people. In the end, though, the message must remain unaltered.

Over the next several weeks, I prayed for Dan as God brought him to mind. Through these times of prayer I became aware of God's desire and intent to use me to lead him to Christ. I knew I needed God's perspective on Dan.

"How would you have me reach Dan with the message of Jesus, Lord?" I asked. Thinking God would give me a revolutionary insight or new evangelistic method, I sat listening for his answer. I waited a long time with no inner response to my prayer, so I turned to the Bible—in opposite order of how things are supposed to be done, as usual.

I thumbed through the gospels, coming across a passage in Luke 11 where Jesus tells a story about a man who has nothing to offer an unexpected guest. The man goes to a friend in the middle of the night and asks to borrow bread, but he gets the cold shoulder. "This is how I feel, Lord," I prayed. "I feel like Dan has come into my life and you've shut the door and aren't giving me anything to go on."

I read on. The man repeatedly asks his friend to lend him some bread, and he finally gets it through his humble persistence. "If you want me to pursue you to borrow some bread that I need for Dan, Lord, I'll ask you every day until I get it," I prayed.

I was determined. It seemed that God had thrown down a challenge, and I wasn't about to give up. I had a sneaking suspicion based on Jesus' story that this was a challenge God wanted to lose. God desired Dan to come into the kingdom much more than I did. God had more at stake here. So why this game?

Here's what I think: God calls us to enduring prayer for lost people to increase our hunger for their salvation. Through this time of prolonged prayer for Dan, I caught a shallow glimpse of God's broken heart for him and that little bit broke my heart too. I began to see him the way God saw him—cold, naked, hungry, confused and futureless. I began to be hungry for his conversion in the same way God was.

When I looked at Dan with my eyes, I saw the exact opposite of what God was allowing me to see with my spirit through prayer. I decided to ignore what I saw with my eyes and rely only on what I saw with my spirit. I no longer saw someone with economic prowess, a well-ordered life and a healthy family; I saw someone on the edge. Dan was on the verge of disaster because he didn't know God and was enslaved to sin, worldly values and the devil. These forces were hidden and their effects not fully visible. The only way I became aware of them was through persistent prayer.

When we acquire God's perspective on people, we simultaneously receive God's purpose and plan to reach them. Now it was clear to me that I had something Dan did not possess—the knowledge of reality. I saw what Dan could not see. I knew and felt what he could not know or feel. Because of my relationship with Jesus, I knew that which was infinitely more important than anything else in Dan's life. I knew the truth.

WITH GOD ALL THINGS ARE POSSIBLE

I had learned three things through my persistence with God in prayer: First, God had the right perspective on Dan and I needed to align my thoughts with his in order to reach Dan. Second, I learned that God desired to let me into his heart by increasing my hunger for Dan's salvation through prayer. Third, I learned that God wanted to bring me to a place of complete trust and dependence on him as I shared the gospel with Dan. In other words, God was inviting me once again to run alongside him in the adventure of seeking a lost sheep.

I was ready to step out in faith to share Christ with a person who didn't look like he had any earthly reason to listen or care.

Dan and I had another appointment scheduled in which I was to sign some paperwork and discuss some of the ideas he had presented at the previous meeting. As I waited for him to arrive, I stood staring into another wintry scene. A blast of Arctic Canadian air had sunk the city into a deepfreeze. Pools of water had frozen in bizarre shapes. Ice hung like poles from rooftops all the way to the ground. The streets were carved ruts of ice, allowing only one car to pass through at a time. It was a time when even Detroit lifers refuse to go outside.

But none of this stopped punctual Dan as he pulled over the ruts and into my salty, crusty driveway. I don't know if it was the prayer or what, but this time my dream car didn't look quite so sleek and sumptuous. Dan didn't walk with the same confident step I was familiar with. His clothes didn't seem as sharply pressed and even his manners seemed to have slipped a notch.

"York, I've highlighted the sections for you to sign," he began abruptly. "Have you made a decision concerning what we talked about last time?"

Dan's brusque tone immediately made me uncomfortable. As I stared at his muscular chin and unblinking crystal eyes, my plans to speak up about Jesus began to waver. "Lord, maybe now isn't the right time," I prayed. "Open a door for me to minister to him if that's your plan."

RECOMMENDED READING

Becoming a Contagious Christian by Bill Hybels and Mark Mittelberg

Right away I sensed God saying back to me, "Now is the time. You walk through the door that's right in front of you and trust me for the results."

I took a deep breath and said the first thing that came to my mind. "Dan, I have something for you to sign too. I'd like you to hear me out on a proposal of my own."

I couldn't believe that corny one-liner had just come out of my mouth. I think Dan knew I didn't mean to start the conversation that way, but he listened anyway. "Sure, I'd be happy to listen to what you have to say," he responded.

As I began to speak, I felt God's presence and power in the room. I spoke with complete confidence, explaining the basic truths of the gospel. Dan sat motionless, staring at the paper I was using to explain the gospel message. As I was talking about how the shed blood of Jesus cleanses us from sin, he stopped me and said, "York, I heard this message when I was a little boy. My mother used to take us to church and I looked forward to each Sunday. When I got older I stopped going, but I could still sense God in my life. I've just never known what he wanted or how to respond to him."

Dan paused for a long time. Eventually he continued, "I knew when I started working with you that there was a reason, and I think this is the reason. What do I do now?"

There it was, the question we all long for—"What must I do to be saved?" The adventure had taken an exciting turn. I hadn't even gotten through the entire message and Dan already wanted to respond to God's love. At that instant I experienced another deep sense of conviction as I realized how I had judged Dan wrong and spiritually written him off in the beginning. God had been working hard in his life and this conversation was the culmination of years of pursuit on God's behalf. I could feel God's pleasure running through me as I spoke on.

"In order to come into relationship with God and have your sins cleansed, you must repent and confess Christ as your leader," I explained. "In order for Jesus to be personally relevant, you must apply his death and the power of his resurrection to your own life. We begin to do this by first agreeing with God that we are sinners and deserve the just penalty of our sin, which is death and hell."

All I had spoken were a few elemental sentences about Christ, but the Holy Spirit was powerfully at work in Dan's heart and his conviction and sense of urgency grew. He murmured, "I know that I'm a sinner. No one has to tell me that." Looking up and speaking louder, he continued, "I understand what you're saying and I'm ready to do this. I've lived my life long enough on my own terms. I want God's way now."

Dan needed to become a follower of Jesus, but there was no denying that he was a leader. He took the lead in the conversation in responding to what he heard. In the same bold and confident way Dan had lived his life, he made a commitment to live for God.

Amid piles of financial documents, Dan and I bowed our heads to pray for God's forgiveness. Though I was inadequate, God had given me his heart for Dan and shown up that day to meet with us. In all the years I have been doing evangelism, there has never been a time that I stepped out in faith when God has not met me more than halfway. In my meeting with Dan, my half-baked comment led to an opportunity that would change his life forever.

RECOMMENDED READING

Developing the Leader Within You by John Maxwell

The Next Generation Leader by Andy Stanley

"What's next?" Dan asked in his businesslike manner after we finished praying. He wanted to get down to business with God and find out exactly what to expect from this newfound relationship.

"Well, Dan," I responded, "the Lord wants you to begin to grow as a man of God. He wants to develop a relationship with you and use you to pass the possibility of relationship with God on to others. Nothing you do now will add to our take away from God's commitment to you, but he has given you several gifts that he expects you to use. He wants to bless you with a new and different kind of life that Jesus called 'abundant living.'"

Each person I help cross the line of faith gets an additional lesson on the importance of prayer, Bible study, the local church and evangelism. I am convinced that these areas of instruction are the best gift we can give a new believer in Christ. When we lead people in making the most important decision of their lives, we must do everything in our power to disciple them. This is difficult for me personally because I'm often on the road and can't meet with large numbers of people from great distances. I can, however, disciple new believers who live near me and try to ensure that those far away are being cared for by partners I work with. I am so serious about this point that I will not come to speak, train or present unless I obtain a written and signed plan detailing how new Christians will be shepherded after my visit. After all, Christ calls us to make disciples, not decisions.

The next Sunday, Dan and his family met us right on time in the foyer of our large Baptist church. They enjoyed the service and Dan's wife said, "I've never seen a priest speak without a robe. I've never seen one in a suit before—it's different."

We went on to our adult Sunday school class for young married couples. The leader asked the group for prayer requests, and to my surprise Dan was the first to raise his hand. "My name is Dan and I'm here with York Moore," he said. "I've recently decided to give my life to God because of York, and I want you to pray for me and my family." A long pause ensued as people stared at us out of the corner of their eyes without turning their heads—an art the Baptists have perfected.

After all the requests were given, we bowed our heads for a time of prayer. Again, Dan was the first to speak. "Dear God, it's me, Dan. I know we haven't talked much lately but you know I'm living for you now. I want to thank you for bringing York into my life to guide me into spirituality and religion. I ask that you would give this pious man the strength to continue spreading Christianity to all the people like me who don't know they're on their way to hell. Thank you."

I think the people in our class were sure I had begun my own little

York Moore cult, but that didn't matter to me. Dan had made his profession public and it was a delight to see him taking steps of faith in prayer and fellowship.

God had again used the adventure of evangelism to touch me and help me grow, as well as to reach a person who was indeed lost and on his way to hell regardless of how he looked, spoke or lived. God grows our faith as we give it away! I am thankful that God called me to a time of listening prayer and confronted me with the need to develop a hunger for Dan. I am thankful that God used Dan to change my heart and teach me not to judge by outward appearances.

APPLICATION

There may be many people like Dan in your life. Perhaps you have been tempted to see them as unreachable. Perhaps you have been intimidated by their pedigree, lavish lifestyle or powerful connections. All these things are window dressings on the souls of people who are going to heaven or hell—these are the only two characteristics that ultimately matter. I would like to challenge you in three areas regarding people of power or influence in your life. First, ask God to give you his divine perspective on them. Ask him to peel back the scales from your eyes and allow you to see with your spirit what's really going on.

Second, I challenge you to learn God's heart for lost people through listening and waiting in prayer. Allow a season of prayer for particular individuals to generate a hunger for their salvation. Ask God repeatedly, daily, perhaps even with fasting, for wisdom and understanding. Don't, however, use prayer as an excuse to not open your mouth and take a risk for God. When speaking with Dan, I almost threw away a great opportunity to see him come into the kingdom of God. Praying for God to open a door is often unnecessary. We live in a sea of opportunities and what we need to do nine times out of ten is to walk boldly through the door in front of us.

Third, I want to challenge you to trust God and depend on him to work in your conversations. Hopefully your opening comments will be more well thought out than mine, but however you do it, the important thing is to start the conversation. Believe that God will meet you more than halfway and take a chance to share the gospel message. Remember to focus on Jesus and what he has done through his death and resurrection. It's also important to invite the person to respond. Like Dan, many people are wondering, *So what do I do now?* We don't need to wait for them to ask; we can spell out what it means to respond to God in faith. You will be amazed not only at what happens in their life but also what takes place in your heart along the way.

11

REACHING PEOPLE UNDER SATAN'S POWER

Large crowds have a life of their own. There's a certain kind of smell to them—a mixture of colognes, perfumes and deodorants (or the lack thereof), along with an aromatic coalescence of carnival foods such as elephant ears, corn dogs and fresh-roasted almonds. Crowds contort and sway like a swarm of migrating birds or a giant living organism undulating atop hot concrete. Crowds also give off a certain sound—a steady hum comprising shouts, whines, murmurs and laughter echoing off buildings and walls. There is an unspoken protocol to a crowd—rules, assumptions and expectations. "Walk on this side of the walkway. Don't look people in the eye for too long. Don't talk to strangers—particularly about God!" Follow these rules and the crowd ripples forward undisturbed; break them and it becomes unhappy and unpredictable.

Walking up a steep slope of concrete in the hot sun, I could hear the rush of just such a crowd. Rounding the corner, I peered into a mass of half-naked, sweating bodies in the city park. Some people lay in the grass reading or listening to headphones. Others galloped after Frisbees or footballs. To my right stood two young men in black suits, looking very much out of place. I sang to myself, "One of these things is not like the others . . ."

The first man was slender and frail but carried himself with assurance and bravado. The other was tall and muscular, like a football player or body builder, yet he seemed less confident. They both were holding up large, leather-bound Bibles as the slender one yelled, "Sinners! Stop sinning! Don't you know you're going to hell?"

I stood under a tree for nearly ten minutes watching and listening to the preacher. Though he was shouting to be heard, he and his companion were just another noisy component of the crowd. People sat around them smoking pipes and rolled cigarettes. Frisbees and footballs whizzed past their heads. Some people stood just inches away carrying on conversations. The preacher was one voice among many, indistinguishable from the rest of the commotion.

I moved closer, intrigued and disturbed by what the man was saying. I chose a spot on the concrete near a yellow park bench. A woman sat on the ground next to me. She was young, perhaps in her early twenties. I studied her as she watched the preacher. Her fingers were burnt-looking and dirty. Sandals revealed swollen toes. She wore a black dress with fringe and beads that hung down past her calves. Several piercings adorned her ears, chin and tongue, out of balance with her manicured makeup and the straight, shiny hair that lay against her olive skin. She was staring intensely at the preacher as he said to a female passer-by, "Whore! Put on some clothes before you burn in the lake of fire!"

The young woman at my feet flicked her cigarette and shouted, "What kind of messed up god you got, buddy?" Except she didn't exactly say "messed" up.

At that moment, my stomach sank deep as pangs of fear and anger struck me. I realized that it wasn't enough for me to sit idly by, analyzing the preacher's message while he shaped the thoughts of others around him. I stared back at the woman as I wondered what to do. I could talk to her, but what about all the other people who had heard the same message? I could talk to the preacher to shut him up, but for many, the damage had already been done. Christ was calling me on the spot to another scary adventure in evangelism. This invitation to join him was immediate, unplanned and could potentially turn hostile. I was trembling, but I had to stand up for God.

I stood on top of the park bench as a wave of fear washed over me. I had done open-air preaching before, but never on the spot without a microphone and at least a plan! I was terrified. "Lord, protect me and use me," I prayed. I felt like I was having an out-of-body experience, like I was standing across the courtyard watching myself. I opened my mouth and words started pouring out.

I shouted to the preacher, "Do you sin?"

Before this moment, the crowd for at least half an hour had been either ignoring the preacher or making fun of him as he shouted at the top of his lungs. I expected the same treatment. But after I yelled this simple question, not only did the preacher turn to face me in disbelief, the entire crowd throughout the courtyard came to a hush.

"I said, do you sin?" I shouted again.

Still no response but deafening silence. I reached into my bag, pulled out my Bible and read 1 John 1:8-10 aloud, which says, "If we say that we have no sin, we are deceiving ourselves, and the truth is not in us. . . . If we say that we have not sinned, we make Him a liar and His word is not in us."

RECOMMENDED READING

Preaching to a Postmodern World: A Guide to Reaching Twenty-First-Century Listeners by Graham Johnston

Turning to the crowd, I continued, "These men use the same words I do, but what they say doesn't make sense. These men are confused about what God has said about sin. More importantly, they are confused about Jesus Christ and what he has done to save us from sin." I began to preach and stood on that park bench for nearly ten minutes as the crowd listened intently.

I preached the law of God, sin, death and judgment. I preached Jesus and him crucified for sin and raised to new life. I preached repentance for the forgiveness of sins. I dipped from the same pool of concepts that the two men had used because no other words and images have the power to save apart from those of Scripture. I had to redeem the words, however, to gather them together and make sense of them, to wash them in a spirit of love and concern, to envelop them in a sense of personal relevance—these were the elements that were missing in the original presentation.

UNCOMMON SENSE

Every Christian has a moral duty to defend the truth and correct error pertaining to Jesus.

Not many of us are called by God to give impromptu sermons to large crowds, but every Christian has a responsibility to correct error and protect the truth from those who distort it. You may not ever get up on a park bench, but in your cafeteria, in the backyard or in a long car ride, you will have opportunities over the course of your life to reverse a great deal of confusion and ignorance pertaining to Jesus. Every Christian must work to defend the faith and correct error. This is not just a job for "the professionals."

In evangelism, people almost always hear our message through a grid of personal experience. Many people's experience with the language of the gospel has produced certain obstacles in their souls. The word *sin* can evoke a host of improper and confused images in the minds of the people we speak with. We must start with the assumption that any given unbeliever holds gross misconceptions about Jesus and then work forward to bring about a proper understanding of the message of Christ. In the United States today, people are either totally oblivious to that message or they have a Frankenstein Jesus in their head that has been spliced together from the media, cults, personal proclivities, parental abuse and so on.

As I preached to the crowd that day, a sense of divine pleasure and assurance flowed through my spirit. I sensed an authority in my words that was absent from the other preacher's message. The crowd sat listening attentively, and not only that, the preachers, particularly the young muscular one, also listened with interest. My oratory skills on this occasion were strikingly substandard—in fact, in that regard I think the cult preachers did a better job. My body trembled as I preached. I often paused to think about what to say next. I didn't know how to end my message. But for all my errors and shortcomings, an otherworldly sense of power and authority emanated from the park bench and it had nothing to do with me.

I finished my sermon by inviting people to pray to receive Jesus and then come forward for further discussion. I spent the next several minutes meeting, counseling and praying with and for people who heard the gospel. The excitement of the moment was surreal until I looked down again at the young woman dressed in black. She had sat at my feet on the concrete near the park bench the entire time, listening and watching. Yet she seemed unimpressed and unmoved, as if a wall of iron surrounded her spirit.

RECOMMENDED READING

Live to Tell: Evangelism for a Postmodern Age by Brad J. Kallenberg

After finishing up with the last person, I turned to the woman and said, "Excuse me, I don't mean to bother you, but I wondered if I could ask you a couple questions."

She looked up at me and squinted in the sunlight, pulling the cigarette from her mouth to say, "I don't know if you really want to talk to me; I'm a practicing witch and a Satanist."

"You're exactly the kind of person I'd like to talk to," I responded. "Do you mind if I sit down?"

She motioned to the space beside her and I sat down on the bare concrete amid the cigarette butts. "I'm York Moore, and you are?"

"Cara," she responded.

"Crazy day here," I said.

"Seems normal to me," she answered. "I've heard it all before. I grew up here and there's a preacher on every block. They all sound the same to me. What you said didn't sound any different from what the other guy said, though I like the way you said it better. I grew up in a Christian home and went to church every week until I got out on my own. My parents shoved this stuff down my throat and now I don't want to have anything to do with it."

All the confidence I'd gained from my park bench experience began to quietly melt away just as the courtyard was clearing and the crowd disbanding.

"I want to hear more about you and your story, Cara," I said. Listening is almost always the best place to start in evangelism, and since I didn't know what else to say I thought it would be a good place to start with Cara.

She talked for a long time about her strict father and subordinate mother, her complacent siblings and overbearing but quaint childhood church. She talked about the comings and goings of all the youth pastors and the relational instability of moral leaders in her life. She spoke of the hypocrisy of her peers and her disappointment in herself for the many immoral decisions she'd made along the way.

More disturbing than what Cara shared was how she shared it. As she chain-smoked and guzzled a liter-sized Pepsi, she spoke of her life as if it were as pointless and insignificant as the cigarette butts blowing around us. She spoke in an eerie, apathetic tone of voice and her stare was dead. I sensed an evil power at work in our conversation and in Cara's life, no doubt brought on by her decision to follow witchcraft. I tried to jar her into focus by asking, "Do you know that Jesus loves you, Cara?"

She continued to stare off and said blankly, "Yeah, I know he loves me. I just don't care."

THE POWER OF PRAYER

As I sat looking at the ground, a cold listlessness came over me. My heart and my skin became chilled as shadows crept over the courtyard walls. My mind was unfocused. I could sense a power at work on me, and I didn't know what to do except pray. I said, "Cara, can I pray for you?"

Cara looked like a deer caught in headlights. She didn't know what to say, and her cigarette dangled dangerously close to her ankles. Young people today may be highly resistant to religious ideology and traditional rhetoric, but they are very spiritual, and open-mindedness is almost a law. Turning down someone's request to pray would come dangerously close to closed-mindedness. "You don't have a problem with me just praying for you, do you?" I continued.

She shook her head and I began to pray. I mean, I prayed! I prayed that God would loose the power of darkness; I prayed against Satan; I prayed for divine protection; I prayed that God would come against every lofty thing that was raising itself against Cara's hearing and understanding of the gospel message. I prayed that God would take the situation captive and allow Cara to be free. I ended by praying, "God, I know that you are more powerful than the enemy, so I pray that you would break through and give Cara ears to hear and eyes to see your love for her today—in Jesus' name!"

As I finished, I fully expected Cara to stand up and walk away, flicking her cigarette butt in my face. My prayer was so offensive, so preachy, so in-your-face that I thought someone like her would scream in disbelief. But she didn't respond that way at all. In fact, Cara simply raised her head, lowered her eyes and leaned forward as I continued.

Without a pause, I finished going over the gospel message. I reviewed all the basics, took a deep breath and asked, "What do you think about all this, Cara?"

In that instant the dam broke, the iron gate was opened and Cara's heart was released. In her first display of emotion since we had begun talking together, she said, trembling, "I want to come to God, but I'm scared."

UNCOMMON SENSE

Without prayer, we cannot speak the gospel in a way that makes an impact against the powers at work in those we are trying to reach.

The Holy Spirit had answered my prayer, breaking through the wall around Cara and me and bringing a supernatural power that enabled her to hear the message of the gospel. As is usually the case, prayer was playing a central role in this evangelistic encounter. The Bible teaches that the gospel, not prayer, is the power of God unto salvation (Romans 1:16). But prayer is our weapon against the powers of darkness. It's our lifeline to God in the tumultuous spiritual sea as we attempt to rescue the drowning from the kingdom of darkness. Prayer gives us the boldness to speak. It gives us the wisdom to hear. It gives us the ability to see. The gospel is the power of God unto the salvation of lost souls, but prayer is God's power to wage war against the world, the flesh and the devil.

We could think of prayer as the cannon from which we aim and shoot and the gospel as the missile we launch. The gospel is the ammunition that breaks down the walls of darkness, freeing the captives, but the cannon of prayer allows us to fire with enough power and accuracy to make an impact. Without prayer, we might as well be trying to throw a thousand-pound artillery shell through a steel-reinforced wall with our bare hands.

Without prayer, we stand alone on the battlefield, naked and exposed, an inviting target for the devil's attacks.

I answered Cara, "There's nothing to be afraid of. Jesus loves you. He's sent me here today to help you understand, truly understand, that truth. Jesus loves you."

Tears began to fall over Cara's smooth skin, smudging her makeup. "It's true that you've heard this message before," I said. "But your freedom depends not on hearing and understanding these truths but on applying them to your soul. Right now, Cara, you're in the fight of your life. You've given yourself to the powers of darkness by worshiping Satan and practicing witchcraft, but even in that state of open hostility to God, he has decided to love you and patiently call you."

RECOMMENDED READING

Fresh Wind, Fresh Fire: What Happens When God's Spirit Invades the Hearts of His People by Jim Cymbala

I continued, "I know you've been hurt by people who were supposedly representatives of God, but right now Jesus and Jesus alone stands before you with hands outspread, calling you home. Does this make sense to you?"

Throwing her cigarette down and placing the cap on her Pepsi, Cara said, "I knew what I was doing was wrong; I could feel God withdrawing from me. I felt cold and afraid, but as I went deeper into witchcraft, I felt less and less. I can hardly feel anything anymore. I want to be free, but I don't know what to do."

Unless we are prepared to answer the "What must I do?" question, all our blood, sweat and tears in evangelism are for nothing. There's no point in telling people about the love of Jesus if we don't also tell them what to do with it. We must call people to action. There is nothing people can do to save themselves, but there is something they must do to allow God to save them—they must repent. Repentance is an opening of the heart, a shift in thinking and a decisive change in volition. To repent means to have a change of heart, which, if genuine, will manifest itself in every area of life—our feelings, our thoughts and eventually our behavior. Genuine repentance begins in the invisible recesses of our hearts and minds and cannot help but spring to life in our actions.

"Cara," I said, "You must repent. To repent means that you say, 'God, I recognize my sin. I recognize the destruction of my choices. I recognize Jesus' death and resurrection on my behalf and I ask for forgiveness and the power to change.' You must also turn and face the reality that nothing you can do will change your life; change must come from God. When you call out to God in this way, Jesus comes and takes you by the hand and walks you out of darkness and into a relationship with him. Over time, you will become more and more like Jesus, more and more righteous, more and more victorious, until one day you will be exactly like him when you are perfected in heaven."

I continued explaining, making sure to stop and ask Cara if she understood before I asked, "Is there any reason why you wouldn't want to repent and ask God to come into your life and walk with you toward right living? Is there any reason you wouldn't want to receive the freeing love of Jesus right now?"

Cara responded, "I would like that very much."

We prayed, asking God for forgiveness and to deliver Cara from the power of witchcraft and the devil. We prayed on the cold concrete, amid the refuse of cigarette butts and an empty Pepsi bottle. We prayed where the crowd had giggled and the preachers roared just hours ago, in that place that had been so full of noise and movement. Though the crowd was gone and the courtyard quiet, there seemed to be more life in that moment of prayer than the entire crowd's heat and swagger. The abundant life of God's kingdom had come in power over one reluctant witch that day.

APPLICATION

We don't like to talk about the devil in these modern days. He's something of a parlor joke, an icon like Uncle Sam or the Skippy peanut butter boy. The devil and his minions have succeeded in luring us into believing that they don't exist, or at least that their presence is innocuous. The truth is that the devil is real. He's as real as the pages you're holding now, as real as the air filling your lungs, as real as the blood pumping through your heart. People who are actively engaged in the warfare of evangelism know this truth better than others, for during the battle Satan can't afford to sit behind smoke and mirrors. He's active and vocal during the moment of rescue and release.

Do you know people whose presence makes you feel unusually tired and cold? Are there situations in which an irrational fear washes over you? Are there times when you feel shut up and restricted from speaking? These are just some of the ways that a spiritual stronghold may be manifesting itself.

Take out a sheet of paper and draw three columns. In the first column, list the ways in which you are aware of the devil's work in your life, in the life of people you know, in your company, your school or your government. After you're done, ask God to illumine your mind. In 2 Corinthians 2:11, Paul says that he and his fellow Christians are not ignorant of Satan's schemes. We don't want to give undue attention to the evil one, but these days that's the least of our errors. Sit for just five minutes and ask God to give you insight into how the devil may be attacking you and the world around you. Add anything to the first column that God has brought to mind.

In the second column, think of thoughtful ways you might pray against each satanic scheme. Where would God have you aim the cannon of prayer against the active work of the devil? Finally, in the third column, list ways God might be leading you to act against the power of the devil. He may be prompting you to approach and speak to someone, to write a senator or city councilwoman, to get involved in a volunteer organization, to give financially to a particular ministry. God may be calling you to stand and publicly defend the gospel's truth from the marauding agents of evil on the park benches of your world. He may be calling you to get dirty and spend some time on the cold concrete with a difficult person. He may be calling you to act in a way that is risky and dangerous.

Whatever God is calling you to do, write it down. Over the next few days, carry this list with you and take a moment or two each day to look it over and pray. Ask God to give you boldness to act in response to what he brings up in your times of prayer, and then do it. Believe that God is more powerful than the evil one and that he will give you what you need to defeat the power of the devil and loose those captive from the kingdom of darkness.

12

REACHING PEOPLE WITH PRACTICAL NEEDS

Since becoming a Christian I have grown increasingly aware that I suffer from a widespread spiritual condition called OPPR, or Other People's Problem Resistance. OPPR causes us to become cold or calloused to the needs of others. Because of it we can flip through 180 channels of satellite television, passing graphic footage of suffering children with bloated bellies, charred skin and sunken eyes without even a flinch. OPPR numbs our hearts, clouds our eyes and deters our actions until it's too late.

I never realized how cold and calloused I was until I became a follower of Christ and began to examine his thoughts, words and actions. Jesus Christ never suffered from OPPR. He hung on the cross with spit running down his leg, covered in baked blood, naked before his own mother because he just couldn't give up on other people's problems—specifically, the problem of sin and the degradation that comes with it.

I became a Christian in the late 1980s in Detroit. This was a depressing time for the city, which was deeply affected by the country's recession. Welfare rolls were at an alarming high, and my family and I were firmly entrenched on them. During the late eighties our meals consisted of government cheese on white bread, canned chicken and water. Food stamps were the most common currency around my neighborhood, often bartered at the back door of the liquor store for cigarettes and soap.

Twenty-one homicides were committed within a mile of my home the year I became a Christian. We lived at the end of a dead-end street where several homes had been boarded up and condemned. There was an active crack cocaine operation just a few doors down, and the air stank of putrid sulfur from the waste disposal plant two blocks away. In these conditions, OPPR was necessary for survival; we could cope only so long with the barrage of death, disease and fear that comes with poverty.

Just a few months after giving my life to God, I was sitting on my front porch reading my Bible when one of the community vagrants walked up to the boarded-up house across the street and sat on the front stoop to drink his forty ounces of malt liquor from a brown paper bag. Typically my brothers and I would have yelled and chased him away from the home to preserve what little dignity we had on our dead-end, crack-infested street, but something happened in my heart that I wrestle with to this day. Instead of feeling anger or fear, my face suddenly flushed, my heart began to pound and my stomach sucked up into my chest. I began to cry as I saw this man through the eyes of Jesus. I saw a lost sheep, alone, vulnerable, afraid, with no one to care for or comfort him.

"God, what should I do?" I prayed.

The Holy Spirit responded, "Give him your shoes."

I've learned over the years that we can usually tell the difference between the Holy Spirit's voice and our own jumbled thoughts because he tells us to do things that challenge us personally. You have to understand that shoes in the 'hood are a big deal. Shoes are one of the few things poor people in the ghetto have. In my neighborhood they were often the reason people get shot, stabbed or mugged. My family couldn't afford bus fare, but I owned a different pair of hundred-dollar tennis shoes for each day of the week. Shoes were personal, shoes were a symbol of pride, shoes were sacred—and here the Holy Spirit was telling me to give this bum my shoes!

Why couldn't God have just continued to allow me to feel all warm and gooey inside? Why couldn't I just have been nice to the bum or given him a quarter? "Why the shoes, Lord?" I asked.

I must have sat there a good ten minutes thinking of all the reasons I couldn't go and offer the man my shoes. *He can't possibly wear the same size as me; what are the chances?* I thought. *If I give him my shoes, I'll never see the end of him. It will only encourage him to come back and take advantage of me.*

Nevertheless, the Holy Spirit kept telling me, "Give him your shoes."

As I walked over to the man, he nervously began to gather his hodge-podge of crinkled papers, plastic bottles and half-smoked cigarettes. "I'm not going to hurt you, sir," I yelled out. "I just want to give you these."

I held up the shoes for him to see, and he smiled and sat back down.

"My name is York, what's yours?" I asked as I shook his clay-like hand.

"Billy. My name's Billy," he responded.

UNCOMMON SENSE

Following Jesus into the adventure of evangelism will frequently cost us personally.

"I don't know if these will fit you or not, but I was just sitting over there at my house reading my Bible and God told me to come over here and give these to you."

Billy smiled, took the shoes and said, "Why, thank you. Aren't you a little young to be a reverend?" He took off his tattered and mismatched loafers and threw them in the bushes.

"I'm not a pastor; I just believe God told me to do this so I'm doing it." As Billy shoved his smelly bare feet into my tennis shoes, I felt defiled. I decided that was enough for one day and ended the conversation.

"I hope they work out for you and God bless you."

I still don't know how the next few words escaped from my mouth. "And if you ever need anything, I live right over there."

I walked back to my porch feeling like I had tumbled down a flight of stairs, hit my head on an end table and was walking around dazed. I didn't know what to think about the feelings of compassion I'd experienced, nor did I know how to feel about the Holy Spirit's clear instruction to give Billy my shoes. I certainly was confused about why I had told him to come by in the future, as if I needed a friend off the streets to come by from time to time and don another pair of my shoes!

That day I came face to face with the profound nature of my calloused condition. It's safer and much more comfortable to ignore and rationalize away other people's problems. Resistance to the voice of our conscience allows us to live in self-indulgence, self-protection and self-worship, but as we come under the control of the Holy Spirit, our hard heart is exposed and the cure is usually a heavy dose of service, risk and obedience. This is what I learned in the adventure of faith that day on the streets with Billy.

The next week, the worst thing that could have happened did. In the middle of the day as I was sitting inside reading the German philosopher Immanuel Kant for a class, someone knocked on my door. When I got to the door, I found Billy staring in the window with a cigarette in one hand and a bottle of beer in the other.

"Hey, Billy. What's going on?" I asked.

"It's like this, Reverend. I gotta catch the bus to appear downtown at court and I need a dollar."

How often have we all heard this line? Immediately we think, *You're not getting on the bus. You're going to go off and buy beer or drugs!* Or, *Sure, I take out my wallet to give you a dollar and you snatch it and run off.*

While these thoughts may lead us to believe that we're actually being more caring and responsible by not giving to people in need, the reality is that self-protective excuses are telltale signs of an OPPR problem. I was still coming to terms with these and other questions myself as a new Christian, but one thing I had decided was that I would no longer turn a blind eye to other people's problems if I had the means to do something. In this case, I did. I reached into my pocket, pulled out two dollars and handed them to Billy.

"Here, get a burger or something on the way," I said. Billy thanked me and quickly went on his way.

About an hour later, I ran up to the store for a study break snack of barbecue pork rinds and Rock and Rye pop—a Detroit favorite! When I turned the corner I saw Billy with yet another bottle of beer sitting in front of the store. My suspicions had been true. He lied to my face and used my money to buy beer and then had the audacity to sit in front of my store and drink it. I was mad, hurt and disappointed.

"Billy, what the heck are you doing? You told me you were going to court and needed my money to get on the bus! What's up with this, man?" My yelling startled him. He hadn't seen me coming, and I hadn't spoken to him in that tone before.

He smiled like a kid caught by his parents in a lie. "Hey man, I don't need this jive from you. I'm going to court, but I'll go when I'm good and ready."

I stormed into the store and out again without even looking at Billy. Returning home, I thought, *If that's what happens when you help people out, I'm not going to have anything to do with it. Lousy bum.*

Again the image of Billy as a helpless sheep without a shepherd entered my mind as the Holy Spirit pressed in with conviction. I wrestled, trying to ignore his words and the conflicting feelings I was experiencing. "Why should I help him, Lord, if all he does is lie and use my money to drink himself to death?"

The Lord answered back, "He's going to have to answer to me for his decisions. I've called you to care for him as you would care for me if I were the one on the street in need."

With that answer, my theology and life instantly changed. For the first time I realized one of the most profound truths in the Christian life. Regardless of other people's responses, their decisions, their reactions or their sentiments, I am called to respond in obedience to God and God alone. In evangelism, this means that despite the fact that people may reject me, may even act with hostility toward me, God has called me to proclaim Jesus to them.

They will have to answer to God for what they do with that proclamation, but I must proclaim! This truth applies not only in evangelism but also in caring for our neighbors, in living moral lives, in deciding how to use our money and time and in dealing with the Billys of our world.

UNCOMMON SENSE

Regardless of what people do with the love and truth we offer, we are responsible to God to give our faith away.

Armed with this new revelation, I was ready for Billy the next time he came around, which didn't take very long. The next day Billy showed up the at my door and had the nerve to ask me again for bus money to get to court.

"Sure, I can help you with that, Billy," I said. He smiled and waited for me to dig into my pocket. Instead I surprised him by stepping outside, closing the door behind us and saying, "I'll go wait at the bus stop with you."

"You don't have to do that, Reverend," he said. "I'm not sure when it's coming."

I responded, "Oh, no problem at all. We can talk as we wait."

As we stood at the bus stop I got to know Billy a little better. I learned that he had been on the street for about three years, that he used to have a family with children and that he worked in the automotive factories until his plant shut down. In those brief twenty minutes I connected with Billy on a deeper level. I said, "I'd like to pray for you and your family if that's all right, Billy."

He looked nervous but replied, "What could it hurt? Go ahead, Rev."

I prayed for a while, thanking God for Billy and for God's love for him before the bus peeked over the horizon.

I saw Billy several times over the course of that spring and summer and had many opportunities to share Jesus with him. Eventually I began to realize that the Lord was using Billy to change me just as much as he was using me to share Christ with Billy. The last time I saw Billy was when I invited him to come to my family's home for Thanksgiving.

"Billy, I see you out here all the time and I know you probably don't have a place to go for Thanksgiving dinner," I said. "I'd like to invite you to join me and my brothers at my mom's house."

But Billy looked hurt, as if I'd said something wrong. "That's real nice, Rev. I don't know what to say."

I told him to come by at one o'clock, and he reluctantly agreed.

My family wasn't too excited about the prospect of a well-known drunk and vagrant coming to our house for Thanksgiving. After some brief explaining on my part (which I realized I should have done beforehand), they agreed that inviting Billy was a good thing. My mother even said, "Well, I guess that's what Thanksgiving is all about. Sure he can come."

Thanksgiving rolled around and the house was filled with all my favorite smells: Mom's ambrosia salad, cheesecake, deviled eggs, ham and burnt biscuits. One o'clock came and went as I stood staring out my window and down the street. Billy never came and I never saw him again. I don't know why he didn't show up. I don't know if, for some reason, Thanksgiving was a painful time for him. He seemed upset at the invitation—I just don't know.

That Thanksgiving meal was bittersweet as I reflected on all I had to be thankful for, much of which I had taken for granted before I met Billy.

I had always concentrated on how poor we were, how little we possessed, how difficult our lives were, but God had used a homeless drunk to change my attitude—not only about my life but about other people's problems.

PREPARE TO CARE

The winter that followed my encounters with Billy was particularly brutal, which was unfortunate for the burgeoning masses of homeless people in Detroit. The governor of Michigan had just signed into law a welfare reform bill that greatly limited funds to impoverished men. As a result, men were hitting the streets in large numbers. At the time my friends from church and I were meeting on Friday nights to debate theology and philosophy in our Dead Theologians Society, patterned after the film *Dead Poets Society* starring Robin Williams.

RECOMMENDED READING

The Cost of Discipleship by Dietrich Bonhoeffer

We took turns choosing books, the only requirement being that the person had to be dead and highly influential in the areas of philosophy and theology. We read Sartre, Kierkegaard and Wittgenstein. We read Calvin, Finney and Stott (we snuck him in even though he wasn't dead). It was a little work of Dietrich Bonhoeffer, however, *The Cost of Discipleship*, that challenged us to couple our endless debates with real and tangible action for the gospel. We decided that every fourth gathering would be an outing to evangelize and care for the needs of real people.

On our first "fourth Friday," all eight of us packed into two small cars and headed downtown to an area that was known as a hangout for vagrants. We parked on the upper deck of a nearby parking garage, prayed for a while and headed down the steps armed with pocketfuls of one-dollar bills. We split into teams of two to share our singles and the gospel with the homeless on the streets. Jerry and I ran into our first homeless man at the bottom of the stairwell of the parking garage.

"Hey, how are you doing?" Jerry began.

"Not too well," the man replied. "I'm kind of hungry, if you know what I mean."

Jerry continued, "Yeah, we were hoping to talk to you about that. Could we buy you a meal?" This question began an adventure that would consume our time, money and hearts for the next several hours.

The man looked at us in disbelief before getting up off the cold concrete. "Virgil's the name, young fellas. What are you doing down here tonight?"

I said, "We've come down here as a part of our club to help some folks out by sharing a meal or two and talking to them about Jesus."

"Well, I never turn down a free meal, so let's go," Virgil said.

We walked two blocks down to a deli shop that served sandwiches and the best baklava in Detroit. While we were walking, Jerry asked Virgil how long he'd been on the street. He responded, "Not too long. Just a couple months since my welfare ran out after the law changed."

Many men were in his same predicament. They weren't hardened drifters but newcomers to the streets, confused and just trying to survive the brutal cold. Most of the missions in the city were overwhelmed and space was limited. Many men had to endure the harsh elements and panhandle on the streets for meal money.

Virgil seemed better-dressed and younger than most of the homeless I was accustomed to speaking with. He might have easily passed as a regular customer in the restaurant if not for the large gash in his black ski jacket and matted hair. As soon as we walked into the deli, however, the woman behind the counter screamed at Virgil, "Get out of here! You're scaring all my customers away!"

I answered quickly, "I'm sorry, ma'am, he's here with us and we were just going to order some food." The woman calmed down and halfheartedly apologized while still glaring at Virgil.

As Virgil chowed down on an enormous pastrami and Swiss sandwich, Jerry and I took turns explaining the gospel. Virgil looked around the restaurant nervously a few times, but he eventually calmed down and began to pay closer attention to what we were saying.

I continued, "Virgil, it was the gift of God in Jesus' death on the cross that allows us to be forgiven of our sins. Does this make sense to you?"

Virgil sensed that I was talking to him like a child and didn't hesitate to point it out. "You think I don't know this stuff? Do you know how many people are down here telling us about Jesus this and Jesus that? Seems like every other day it's another one of you guys telling us this as if I ain't ever been to church. Shoot [except he didn't say shoot], I used to go to church all the time. But if God is so loving, then why am I out here on the street?"

Without missing a beat Jerry answered, "I can't begin to understand what you've been through, Virgil. I'm very sorry for the situation you're in. If you're interested, though, we do have some things to say about that."

UNCOMMON SENSE

Caring for people physically is not at odds with caring for them spiritually.

Virgil seemed intrigued; no one had ever taken time to get involved with the messy details of his life. I said, "I know this doesn't answer all your questions about how a loving and all powerful God could allow evil and suffering, such as your situation, but this is how we can at least begin to think about it. First, God does see and care about your situation. The Bible teaches that God responds in three ways to evil and suffering. First, God is moved by our suffering. For example, when Jesus goes to the tomb of his dead friend Lazarus, he weeps. God sees your situation and he weeps as you suffer."

Virgil looked as if this were the first time he'd ever heard anything like this.

I continued, "However, a God that simply cries in the face of suffering is weak and impotent. The Bible says that our God takes action. When Jesus went to the cross to die, he took onto himself the sins of the world. Jesus died to bring an end to sin and its reign of evil. It's through the death and the power of the resurrection of Jesus that we can begin to turn the great evils of our world upside down, including the evil of poverty and homelessness. That's why we're down here tonight, hoping to have at least some kind of impact with our time and money on the lives of real people."

I concluded by saying, "Virgil, a God who merely cries and dies is no kind of God at all. The Bible adds that one day Jesus Christ will return to judge the world and bring a new kingdom of righteousness. He'll bring an end to suffering, political injustice, poverty and racial strife. God's ultimate solution for evil and suffering is to do away with it entirely. Does this make sense to you?"

Jerry and I were used to dialogue and debate, and because Virgil's questions dealt with the ultimate issues of evil and suffering, we assumed he was interested in the same kind of discussion. His response showed otherwise. Virgil threw his sandwich down, hung his head in his hands and wept bitterly. Through sobs he asked, "Why do you all care? Ain't nobody ever stopped to talk to me or take me out to lunch. They just throw their money at me or holler something about Jesus or give me a pamphlet, but you all really care. Why?"

Jerry answered, "We care about you because Jesus cares about you. We love you because we love Jesus."

Virgil cried for a good three or four minutes before we continued speaking. "Virgil, we believe Jesus has sent us to you to tell you that he sees, he cares and he has a plan for your life that begins with you letting him take control," I said. "We don't know what the next step is to get you off the street, though we definitely want to help make that happen. What we do know is that the next step for your situation is to ask Jesus to forgive and cleanse your sin and ask him to take control of your life. Is that something that you want to do today?"

It didn't take long for Virgil to answer, "I want that more than anything. I know I need the Lord."

We prayed with Virgil as the deli counter girl glared at us holding hands over a half-devoured pastrami and Swiss sandwich.

APPLICATION

How are you doing with your OPPR condition? Do you have a high resistance to other people's problems? Do you find yourself using a well-stocked armory of excuses as to why you can't or shouldn't get involved in the lives of people with needs? Let me challenge you to give financially and to give generously to organizations that provide large-scale care and protection for the poor and powerless of our world. At the same time, it's often too easy to just write a check. We also have to get involved in the lives of real people. We must help suffering children overseas and give canned goods to the local food pantries, but we must also get involved with the messy business of face-to-face interaction and assistance.

RECOMMENDED MINISTRIES

The International Justice Mission

<www.ijm.org>

World Vision

<www.worldvision.org>

Those of us who are part of the world's wealthiest country have an extra burden to give our time, energy, resources and money to help people who are in need. Biblical evangelism requires both that we proclaim Christ and that we make personal contact with people in need. Giving to missions and ministries can never take the place of sacrificing our own time, energy and personal security.

Getting involved in the lives of others is not only a biblical mandate, it's also a part of God's wonderful adventure to make us more like his Son, Jesus. It was through my yielding to the Holy Spirit's voice to give Billy my shoes that I came to understand the hardness of my heart. It was through that understanding that I was able to repent and change the way I thought and felt toward those in need. As I began to research why so many men were homeless, I started to understand that a pocket filled with dollars was not the ultimate solution, but it was a start, at least for me. What is the start for you? We all have Billys and Virgils in our lives; we all have real and practical needs before us. Often, however, we have to ask God to do radical surgery on our spiritual eyes so that we can see what we have become skilled at screening out.

The American church, unfortunately, tends to dichotomize the biblical mandate to care for the poor, hungry, homeless, widows and orphans of our world from the mandate to proclaim Christ. We cannot do one without the other. To care for the physical needs of people while refraining from preaching Christ is to place a warm coat on the back, nourishing food in the stomach and shoes on the feet, and then push the entire soul headlong into hell. At the same time, to proclaim Christ while ignoring real physical needs is to bellow forth empty words that swish about ineffectively, doing more to help people into hell than our silence ever could.

RECOMMENDED READING

Good News About Injustice

by Gary A. Haugen

In what way can you help at least one real person this week hear the good news of Jesus through your care and service? I'm not telling you to perform a random act of kindness, but rather to couple your proclamation of the gospel with real, costly and involved service to another human being. Because of the insidious nature of hardheartedness, you might have to spend a significant amount of time thinking and praying for the ability to even see such an opportunity. But I guarantee that if you ask, God will open your eyes.

This kind of service might mean spending time with a lonely widow or shut-in. It might mean going to a local hospital, orphanage or jail and visiting people who are locked down and forgotten by society. It might mean filling your pockets with dollars and going to that place in town where you don't ever go intentionally to see the people you try so hard not to see. It might mean inviting those needy and awkward neighbors over for an evening of dinner and dialogue. Whatever it is, ask God to deal with your OPPR condition, take the risk to step out in faith, and get involved in the life of a real person.

13

REACHING ANYONE GOD
BRINGS OUR WAY

Welcome aboard," the captain of the plane said as the mass of human flesh pressed toward their seats, making pit stops along the way to stow luggage that should have been checked in the first place. By the time I arrived at the very last seat in the rear of the plane, all the super-extra-small airplane pillows had been taken and both bathrooms were lit up with the "occupied" sign. My head and bladder were pounding with every heartbeat.

"At least I don't have to sit by anyone," I sighed. The seat next to me was not assigned and I was already loosening my belt and relaxing my legs in the extra space.

As the door closed and the plane started making quirky, grinding noises, my stomach joined my nerves in open rebellion and I recalled just how much I hated to fly. Hot flashes, cold flashes, nausea, shortness of breath—panic would set in from the moment I ordered my tickets over the Internet and not let up until the wheels came screeching down at my "final destination." I hated to fly, so why was I on this plane with all these annoying people? Because I had just finished a wonderful week of training and networking at a national conference for evangelists in the South. As is often the case after such experiences, however, I was ready to turn off the evangelistic juice and tune out.

A few rows forward, a shuffle drew my attention. I looked up and saw the flight attendant pointing a tall, well-dressed man right at me. *Great. Here goes my empty seat*, I thought. Sure enough, the man walked directly to the seat next to me and explained how the flight attendant wanted him to move in order to place a child with her mother. I squeezed out a half-hearted, "Welcome!" as I moved my feet into the breadbox-shaped compartment in front of me. We exchanged the normal in-flight pleasantries.

"My name's Urich," he said. "What's yours?"

"York. Good to meet you." Was it really good to meet him? Not really, but that's what social convention dictated I say.

"Are you down here for business or pleasure?" he asked.

This question inevitably gets me into a conversation about Jesus. It's funny how social convention can keep us from sharing Jesus in some contexts and force us to do so in others. I answered, "I'm an evangelist and I've been down here attending a conference for evangelists from around the country."

I figured a straightforward answer with just the right sprinkling of religious words would scare him into silence, and sure enough it did. Urich responded, "That's interesting," and stopped speaking as the plane jerked forward a few feet on the runway.

On one hand I was relieved by Urich's silence. The flight was only about an hour long and I intended to ride it out in silence. On the other hand, however, I was uneasy in my conscience. This kind of restlessness usually meant the Holy Spirit was pressing in on me, calling me to obedience and action. God wanted to grow and stretch me. God had another leg of the adventure for me to engage in on that plane. But I was too preoccupied with myself to be open to it right away.

We often turn away from the gentle prodding of the Holy Spirit. When we consistently do so, we grow calloused and unable to detect his voice. We grow confused about whether we're just feeling uncomfortable, whether it's appropriate to do something, or whether we need to take a step of faith to share Jesus. There are often weeks and even months when this is the case in my life. I allow myself to go on vacation, so to speak, from God's daily leading. I want to tune out the Holy Spirit's voice because living in the daily adventure is, in a word, tiring. It takes fresh faith and energy to engage with God every day. At that point on the plane with Urich, I just wasn't "feelin' it." Jesus, however, as he is prone to do, jolted me back into the adventure.

As our plane taxied on the runway, I noticed a long line of planes in front of us waiting to take off. Just then the captain announced, "Due to weather conditions, we've been placed in a hold for takeoff. We apologize for any delay this may cause."

Just my luck! No pillow, no bathroom, no leg room, and now I was stuck on the runway with a guy whose name I could hardly pronounce. I balled up my coat, jammed it behind my head and tried to fall asleep. As I sat there, the Holy Spirit continued to work on my heart. I began to ask myself why I didn't care about these people on the plane. Why was I so annoyed by the situation? Was there a divine reason why this guy was sitting next to me?

Random questions continued to run through my head until the Holy Spirit brought an image from Scripture to my mind. I recalled Jesus spending time with a convert named Levi. I pictured Jesus at Levi's house as people began showing up for a "coming out" party of sorts. Levi was a new Christian and had invited a great crowd to his home so he could introduce them to Jesus. Levi had a fresh love for Jesus. Levi had a vision for the people in his life. Levi was taking risks. I was not like Levi. As my physical discomfort grew, so did my spiritual restlessness.

I began to think about my early days as a Christian. I never used to feel too tired and spent to tell someone about Jesus. I remember a time when every chance encounter was an opportunity too great to pass up. I remember the sense of adventure and excitement. I remember the sense of challenge and risk. I remember a time before I entered professional ministry and began attending conferences on evangelism when I was more like Levi. One of the great tragedies of the Christian life is the trend away from freshness and risk as we get "professional" about our faith. It seems that the more serious and fluent we are in our dialogue with Jesus, the less risky and childlike we are in our faith. Why is this? Shouldn't it be the opposite?

As I thought these thoughts the Holy Spirit pressed in again, further and deeper into the hardness of my heart. God was calling me to have grace in this situation—to be helpful and show goodwill, or to bestow unmerited favor, as the Bible defines grace. I had received grace upon grace from God in

---

RECOMMENDED READING

What's So Amazing About Grace?
by Philip Yancey

---

my own life. He had shown goodwill to me. He had granted me unmerited favor and benevolent action, and now he was calling me to do the same for Urich as we sat stalled on the runway.

God brought a saying of Jesus to my mind: "I have not come to call righteous men but sinners to repentance" (Luke 5:32). Jesus defined his coming, his very presence in the lives of people around him, as a gracious voice calling sinners to repentance. I muttered to myself with my eyes closed and my body slumped against the window. "I am not here on this plane to call the righteous, but Urich to repentance." I was reluctantly hooked back into chasing after Jesus into the adventure.

I sat up and began to engage with Urich. "I never asked what you did for work."

Urich explained that he was an engineer for a German company working on an automotive project. I asked, "What's the general perception among Germans of evangelists?" I've found that most people's perceptions of the effectiveness, integrity and motives of evangelists fall on the extreme negative end of the spectrum.

"Well, we don't really have evangelists in Germany," Urich answered. "Just the ones on TV, and they always talk about money."

He continued, "I was raised Lutheran and took the required religious classes in school. In Germany religion is everywhere, but it has its place. You see, we Germans don't take religion terribly seriously, so we are neither offended nor impassioned by it as you Americans are." I detected a hint of pride in his voice.

Looking out the window, I saw the first planes around the corner beginning to take off. Just then the captain announced, "We've been cleared for takeoff and as soon as it's our turn on the runway, we will begin our flight."

I knew I had just about an hour now to navigate a conversation with Urich. I wished I had more time. I wished I had not wasted precious minutes trying to ignore my seatmate. I wished I had come onto the plane with a heart ready to notice and engage with whoever came my way. I needed desperately to redeem the time.

REDEEMING THE TIME

"Why do you think Germans are less passionate about religion, Urich?" I asked.

He answered, "We are a people who have seen a lot of fanaticism in our country, and it is looked down upon as extreme and sometimes dangerous. We feel like religion needs to be a part of our society and culture but kept in check so we don't get fanatical about it."

I reflected on Urich's answer awhile and then tried to re-articulate his comments. "So, if I understand you correctly, you are saying that religion, like the postal service or the grocery store or the gas station, is a common element in the German cultural landscape but that it's kept under control by certain social conventions and expectations so that it does not assume an overcentralization in people's lives?"

"That is exactly right," he said with a smile.

Before I could get the next sentence out, our plane began to roar, taking to the air sideways. I clenched my teeth and grabbed hold of both armrests as I thrust my back firmly into my seat. "I hate to fly," I said.

Urich looked at me a bit surprised and then tried to set me at ease. "I make this flight every week," he said. "There's nothing to worry about. We'll be on the ground in exactly one hour and eight minutes."

His relaxed tone and expression did indeed help me calm down. I have found that when I allow someone to help me by assisting with some heavy lifting or getting my mail when I'm out of town or comforting me on a plane, that person is much more open to what I have to say. If we as Christians think we need to serve all the time and never allow the lost to serve us, we make a grave error. People want to serve, even if it's sometimes for the wrong reasons. Also, when we attempt to serve others without allowing them to serve us, issues of power and manipulation can arise, making people question our motives. But when we invite people to help us or are transparent with our weaknesses and needs, people tend to jump in eagerly. We need to serve and love others in our evangelism, but we also need to make room for others to serve and care for us.

"Urich, can I ask you some questions about your understanding of God?" I said.

"Sure. I like talking about religion," he responded.

I began by asking him what he thought of Jesus Christ.

"To be honest with you, I've never thought about that," he said. "I believe he was born of a virgin, died on the cross for sins and then rose from the dead on the third day, but I don't have any personal opinion about him."

Urich had accurately explained in a nutshell the good news of the gospel before I could even share it with him, but although he spoke correctly, it was what he didn't say that concerned me. Urich had a proper religious education that included the historic facts about Jesus of Nazareth, but he did not actually know Jesus. A frequent mistake we make when sharing our faith is to assume that people who know what we're talking about actually know Jesus personally. Another mistake is to assume that since they know the facts about Jesus, we can't do anything to move them forward in entering into a relationship with Jesus. These assumptions could not be further from the truth.

"It sounds like your religious education in Germany was not wasted," I affirmed. "I would like to share a couple things and get your impressions about them, if that would be all right."

Urich seemed intrigued and sat up to watch as I began to scrawl out some words and pictures on a napkin on the fold-out tray in front of me. As I began, I glanced at my watch. Only thirty-five minutes to go.

"The first thing I want to explain, which you've already alluded to, is that Jesus came to die on the cross for our sins," I said. "Sin is more than wrong actions and thoughts. Those things are just manifestations of a disease, the disease of sin. God cares about our sickened condition and knows that we are in need of radical treatment. The disease of sin can't be fixed by going to church, reading the Bible or even getting a good religious and moral education."

RECOMMENDED READING

The Master Plan of Evangelism

by Robert E. Coleman

Urich looked puzzled. "Then why do any of those things if they don't help?"

I answered, "That's a very good question. It all depends on what those things represent for you. You can read your Bible in order to seek to appease a guilty conscience. You can go to church because you think it will earn you a higher grade in heaven. You can learn about Jesus to fulfill a scholastic requirement or meet the social expectations of your culture. All of these reasons do absolutely nothing for your soul, however."

"Urich," I continued, "God is real and he loves you, but if your own determination or religiosity could make you a better person, don't you think it was kind of stupid for God to send Jesus to the cross to die?"

He answered, "I never thought about it that way before."

As I went to continue, the plane dropped and jerked. The passengers started to mutter and look nervously out the windows, and I again gripped my seat. I thought to myself that if the plane went down and I perished in the crash, there was nothing I would rather be doing than talking to Urich about Jesus as it happened. What a long distance I had come in just under an hour. How I had longed for Urich to mind his own business, how I had longed to sit by myself, how I had longed to be off the plane. All that had changed now. The words of Jesus were still ringing in my ears. "I have not come to call the righteous but sinners to repentance."

I jumped back into the conversation. "Urich, you said rightly that Jesus died for our sins. I want you to know that when Jesus hung on that cross, he did so voluntarily in order to turn the wrath of God away from us. Even though God loves us, he must judge our sin because he is holy. Jesus hung on the cross, absorbing the punishment that was coming our way, and if we apply his death to ourselves, all the wrath and condemnation that is rightfully ours will have been taken care of so that we can enjoy friendship with God."

The plane began to descend as my ears started popping and the flight attendant collected empty cups and crinkled pretzel bags. I had just a few more minutes with Urich. He asked, "So how do you do that? How do you apply Jesus' death to your own sin?"

UNCOMMON SENSE

Engaging in the adventure of evangelism will reignite our hunger both for Jesus and for his lost sheep. Doing often precedes feeling.

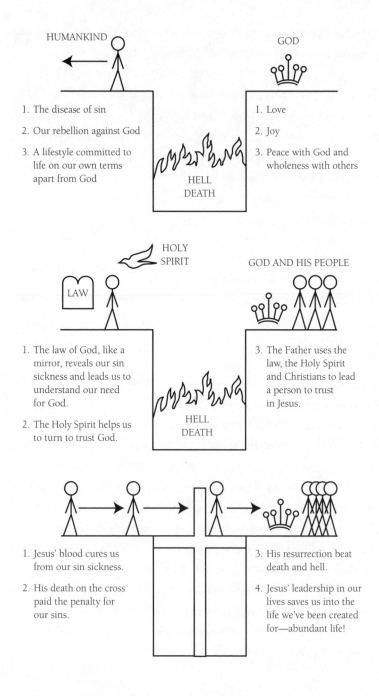

HUMANKIND

GOD

1. The disease of sin

2. Our rebellion against God

3. A lifestyle committed to life on our own terms apart from God

HELL
DEATH

1. Love

2. Joy

3. Peace with God and wholeness with others

HOLY
SPIRIT

GOD AND HIS PEOPLE

LAW

1. The law of God, like a mirror, reveals our sin sickness and leads us to understand our need for God.

2. The Holy Spirit helps us to turn to trust God.

HELL
DEATH

3. The Father uses the law, the Holy Spirit and Christians to lead a person to trust in Jesus.

1. Jesus' blood cures us from our sin sickness.

2. His death on the cross paid the penalty for our sins.

3. His resurrection beat death and hell.

4. Jesus' leadership in our lives saves us into the life we've been created for—abundant life!

I continued to sketch out my picture and explain the gospel as Urich sat with his eyes riveted to the napkin.

"The Bible talks about repentance," I began.

He interjected, "That's when you say you're sorry for something, right?"

"That's part of it, but let me give you a three-dimensional view. Imagine that you're walking down a grassy slope with an easy and steady decline. Each step you take, however, gets steeper and steeper, deeper and deeper into a dark ravine, darker and darker until you find yourself far down a mountainous path. As you look ahead, you see glowing embers of fire, you hear screams of despair, you sense danger. You look over your shoulder and see miles of sheer rock—it's impossible to backtrack. Repentance first means you realize the danger you're in and that your own actions have led you down this path."

RECOMMENDED READING

The Cross of Christ by
John Stott

As I drew the curvy hill and flames, Urich's face crumpled a bit and the hydraulic motors of the wings whirled.

I continued, "Second, repentance means you recognize that if you continue on the path you're on, you will certainly meet God's judgment. Third, and most importantly, repentance means you call up to the one person who has never gone down the path of sinful rebellion, the righteous Son Jesus Christ. When you call to Jesus, you're saying to him that you recognize his righteousness and the fact that his death on the cross is the only solution to save you from the path you're on. When you do this, Jesus comes into that dark and hopeless place and saves you. You're saved from sin, death and future condemnation. What do you think about this, Urich?"

Urich thought a long time, looking down as we were instructed to return our seats to their "upright and locked positions." Urich spoke low and seriously. "When I was a teenager, I did some things that I knew were wrong in God's eyes. I felt deeply that I had disappointed God. I remember feeling distant and cold from an important presence in my life. My life has continued to be cold and distant until now."

Looking up, he continued, "I know that this message is for me. I know that Jesus died for me. I want to apply his death to my sin."

By now, the flight attendant was strapped into her jump seat behind us and was listening to our every word. I could see the buildings on the ground appearing. I had only a few moments, so I said, "Urich, God longs for that. I would like to pray a simple prayer with you that acknowledges your desire to be forgiven and your belief in the death of Jesus for your sin. Can we do that together?"

Urich answered without hesitation and with the same excitement he had initially showed in our conversation. What a wonderful turn he made away from pride, self-reliance and comfort, a turn from social convention and tradition—a turn to Jesus Christ. Urich repeated the words after me as the wheels squawked on the runway and the plane hopped and jerked. "Jesus, forgive me; I am a sinner. I believe you died on the cross in my place. I believe you beat death and sin when you rose from the dead. Come into my life and lead me away from destruction and into life with you and your people. In Jesus' name, Amen."

As we ended, I looked at my watch. One hour, eight minutes exactly.

APPLICATION

In my postconference weariness, I had assumed that I was on break from taking notice of the people in my life. I had made up my mind that I would not be disturbed by others. In so doing, I had relegated the mass of people around me to a level of annoyance and inconvenience. I had "thingafied" the lost sheep of Jesus and had slipped into a state of unconcern.

This attitude of my heart was sin. It was faithlessness. It was selfishness. Jesus took time out of his busy schedule to spend real time with

Levi. He never took a break from noticing people in his life. He did take time alone to be with God in prayer, but in those sublime times of intimacy he recaptured the joy and courage to care for people.

Social convention works against our sharing Jesus more than it does to facilitate it. Understanding this, are there specific people in your life you've avoided sharing Jesus with because it seemed too awkward? Perhaps others might overhear your attempts. Perhaps it would seem inappropriate in a particular setting. Whatever the reason, don't let social convention stop you from making a difference in the life of someone who desperately needs God's forgiveness and love.

Spend some time reflecting on the past week. Bring the days' events into your mind's eye. The store, the post office, the dinner party—have you been more concerned with your own comfort, your own time, your own agenda, your own needs? Have you been more concerned about people's perception of you? Have there been Levis who slipped through the cracks of your attention because of fear or weariness? Listen to the Holy Spirit. What might he say about your week? How might Jesus have lived your week differently had he been in full control? As the plane of your life bumps and drops, as the iron gate of social convention closes around you, as your own needs eclipse those of the people right under your nose, remember the words of Jesus: "I have not come to call the righteous but sinners to repentance."

UNCOMMON SENSE

There is never a time when we are off duty, and often when we think we are, Jesus chooses to lead us into another adventure of faith and risk.

CONCLUSION
Developing a Plan

The adventure of evangelism is something we do with Jesus, not merely for Jesus. Many times we hear the words of the Great Commission as a "go" into all the world to make disciples instead of a "join me as I go," as it was intended. We need to recognize that the final verses of Matthew 28 are just as much an invitation as a commissioning. Look afresh at the words of Jesus: "God authorized and commanded me to commission you: Go out and train everyone you meet, far and near, in this way of life, marking them by baptism in the threefold name: Father, Son, and Holy Spirit. Then instruct them in the practice of all I have commanded you. I'll be with you as you do this, day after day after day, right up to the end of the age" (Matthew 28:18-20 *The Message*).

What could be more exciting than joining Jesus in what he does every day? Jesus' Palm Pilot, if he had one, would be full of appointments with lost people. Our calendars need to by hot-synced, if you will, with Jesus' agenda. Just after I became a Christian, two of my buddies and I founded a chapter of Campus Crusade for Christ at our college. Through the little pamphlet *The Four Spiritual Laws* I first became acquainted with the phrase "God has a wonderful plan for your life." Over the years I have found that God really does have a wonderful plan for my life and it primarily focuses on the adventure of joining Jesus in his mission to seek and save the lost.

I want to issue some final recommendations and challenges. First, I encourage you to leaf back through the pages of this book and briefly inventory the "Uncommon Sense" entries; these will provide a good overview of what you've learned. If you recorded illustrations of how these truths have played out in your life as I recommended in the introduction, allow some time to reflect on these experiences. Think about what the next steps for growth could look like in each area.

Second, I have recommended twenty-seven books and other resources. If you can, obtain the resources as reference guides and attempt to read two of the books a month for the next year. This might seem like quite a challenge, but believe me, these materials are worth the investment of finances and time. If you are a slow reader like me, you might want to read one of the books a month for the next two years.

The main point is to develop a plan for growth. Just as it says in chapter seven, we will never grow as witnesses with a "somehow, some way" plan. Many people give little attention to how they will sharpen their skills as God's witnesses and effectively engage in the adventure. Make a plan and stick with it. I've provided one plan, but if this doesn't fit you or your lifestyle, make another one. Ask yourself, "What books can I read? What conferences can I go to? What steps of faith can I take? How can I grow in reliance on God in the journey?" However you answer these questions, develop a plan for growth in the adventure.

Third, I challenge you to develop a book of stories about your own journey in the adventure. They don't all have to be success stories, as I have illustrated. The stories that you record should share what you have learned and how you have grown as a result of following Jesus into the adventure. How have you grown as you've attempted to give your faith away? What risks have you taken? What was the result? In what areas do you need to continue to grow to become a mature witness?

Finally, I want to encourage you to pass this book along to others. Don't just put it on the shelf to collect dust but let it challenge and free someone you care about—why not give it away? If you've recorded personal thoughts or plans in the margins, why not buy a copy of this book for a close friend as a gift? You can also continue to use this book by reading it with a small group of friends. Reading two chapters a week and gathering to discuss their application and relevance to your life is an excellent way to grow with other believers. Leading a discussion group could also help you become a leader in the adventure, helping others experience the joy that comes with living on the edge of faith. However you use the book, I challenge you to just keep on using it.

Commission and invitation go hand in hand. Jesus sends every one of his witnesses into the world, and he invites us to join him in the awesome, scary, risky, costly adventure that is evangelism. The invitation is for every Christian, not just the "professionals." Whether or not you were aware of it at the point of your own conversion, becoming a follower of Jesus is simultaneously a call to be his witness, his co-adventurer. Engage in the adventure. Learn to love the adventure. Press into the adventure, being honest about fears and failures, mistakes and misgivings, tears and trials. God promises to grow and mature you as a Christian throughout it. May he bless you as you become his bold adventurer.

RECOMMENDED READING LIST

Blackaby, Henry, and Claude V. King. *Experiencing God: Knowing and Doing His Will*. Nashville: Lifeway Christian Resources, 1990.

Bonhoeffer, Dietrich. *The Cost of Discipleship*. New York: Touchstone, 1959.

Chapman, Colin. *Cross and Crescent: Responding to the Challenge of Islam*. Downers Grove, Ill.: InterVarsity Press, 2003.

Coleman, Robert. *The Master Plan of Evangelism*. Grand Rapids: Revell, 1994.

Cymbala, Jim. *Fresh Wind, Fresh Fire*. Grand Rapids: Zondervan, 1997.

The Essential IVP Reference Collection: The Complete Electronic Bible Study Resource. Downers Grove, Ill.: InterVarsity Press, 2003.

Grenz, Stanley. *Welcoming but Not Affirming*. Louisville: Westminster John Knox, 1998.

Haugen, Gary. *Good News About Injustice*. Downers Grove, Ill.: InterVarsity Press, 1999.

Hybels, Bill, and Mark Mittelberg. *Becoming a Contagious Christian*. Grand Rapids: Zondervan, 1994.

Johnston, Graham. *Preaching to a Postmodern World: A Guide to Reaching Twenty-First-Century Listeners*. Grand Rapids: Baker, 2001.

Kallenberg, Brad. *Live to Tell: Evangelism for a Postmodern Age*. Grand Rapids: Brazos, 2002.

Maxwell, John. *Developing the Leader Within You*. Nashville: Thomas Nelson, 1993.

Moore, Beth. *Believing God*. Nashville: Broadman & Holman, 2004.

Nelson's Electronic Bible Reference Library. Nashville: Thomas Nelson, 1997.

Ortberg, John. *If You Want to Walk on Water, You've Got to Get Out of the Boat*. Grand Rapids: Zondervan, 2001.

Pippert, Rebecca Manley. *Out of the Saltshaker*. Downers Grove, Ill.: InterVarsity Press, 1999.

Plantinga, Cornelius, Jr. *Not the Way It's Supposed to Be*. Grand Rapids: Eerdmans, 1995.

Richardson, Rick. *Evangelism Outside the Box*. Downers Grove, Ill.: InterVarsity Press, 2000.

Schaeffer, Francis. *The Mark of the Christian*. Downers Grove, Ill.: InterVarsity Press, 1970.

Spurgeon, Charles Haddon. *Soul-Winner: How to Lead Sinners to the Saviour*. Grand Rapids: Kregel, 1995.

Stanley, Andy. *The Next Generation Leader*. Sisters, Ore.: Multnomah Publishing, 2003.

Stiles, Mack. *Speaking of Jesus: How to Tell Your Friends the Best News They Will Ever Hear*. Downers Grove, Ill.: InterVarsity Press, 1995.

Stott, John. *The Cross of Christ*. Downers Grove, Ill.: InterVarsity Press, 1986.

Sweet, Leonard. *SoulTsunami*. Grand Rapids: Zondervan, 1999.

White, John. *Daring to Draw Near*. Downers Grove, Ill.: InterVarsity Press, 1977.

Wilkinson, Bruce. *The Prayer of Jabez*. Sisters, Ore.: Multnomah Press, 1984.

Yancey, Philip. *What's So Amazing About Grace?* Grand Rapids: Zondervan, 2002.

For more information about York Moore, his ministry and resources, or to contact York about a speaking engagement, visit <www.tellthestory.net>.